UNSPOKEN

The Scopes Trial and the
Undelivered Speech of
William Jennings Bryan

Alton L. Gansky

UNSPOKEN

The Last Speech of William Jennings Bryan

Alton Gansky

alloyd

Unspoken:

The Last Speech of Williams Jennings Bryan

Copyright © 2016 by Alton Gansky

Published by Alloyd Books
(Gansky Communications)

ISBN 10: 1535346922
ISBN 13: 978-1535346924

All rights reserved. No part of this book may be reproduced without written permission, except for brief quotations in books and critical reviews.

Scripture quotations by the author are taken from the New American Standard Bible®, Copyright © 1960, 1962, 1963, 1968, 1971, 1972, 1973, 1975, 1977, 1995 by The Lockman Foundation Used by permission." (www.Lockman.org)

Scripture quoted by William Jennings Bryan in his speech are drawn from the King James Version

TABLE OF CONTENTS

Author's Forward

About this Book

1925: Scopes "Monkey Trial"

Text of Speech with Annotation

A Brief Reply by Clarence Darrow

About the Author

Endnotes

AUTHOR'S FORWARD

THE TENNESSEE SUMMER of 1925 was stifling. Still, hundreds of people of Dayton, Tennessee and nearby regions came dressed in suits and dresses to stand along the tracks where a Southern Railways train waited. Men, several in Navy uniforms, carried a bronze coffin to the back of the last car and helped load a passenger well-known to the entire country. It was July 29, and the man in the coffin had died in his sleep three days before. The man was sixty-five-year-old William Jennings Bryan, one of the best known men of his day and one of the most controversial figures in U.S. history.

The train moved south from the now famous berg to Chattanooga approximately forty-five miles away, then turned north to make the 600-mile journey to the nation's capital. Along the way the train made stops and crowds gathered to pay their respects. Hymns were sung, men and women wept, and some peered through the back door of the railcar to catch a glimpse of the Great Commoner—a door Mary Baird Bryan, the deceased's wife, had requested be left open so people could peek inside. Had the news not already been widely spread, an onlooker seeing the emotional crowds might be forgiven for thinking the president of the United States had died.

William Jennings Bryan was a polarizing force in politics during the late nineteenth and early twentieth century. Although often described as a self-aggrandizing, publicity-seeking, ignorant, religious bigot, he was nothing like that portrayal. He was a man passionate about fairness, faith, and the common man. He spent over thirty years in politics winning many to his thinking and aggravating some to the point of hatred. No one was ambivalent about WJB.

His résumé is almost too much to believe: lawyer, international traveler, orator, congressman. At thirty-six, he was the youngest man to run for president. He went on to become a publisher, platform speaker, Bible teacher, Presbyterian leader, contributor to three constitutional amendments, secretary of state under Woodrow Wilson, and author. He was the first presidential candidate to take his message directly to the people. In his day, candidates let others campaign for them. It was considered undignified to do otherwise. WJB chose to ignore the custom and make his case directly to the voters, traveling thousands of miles by train and car. Wherever he went, hundreds showed up to hear the man from Nebraska speak.

Today most only remember two things about William Jennings Bryan: his "Cross of Gold" speech, and what has become known as the "Scopes Monkey Trial." The Cross of Gold speech launched Bryan into the public spotlight and so moved his fellow Democrats that they made him their candidate for president in the 1896 election. It is a speech that can be found in most books listing the country's greatest orations.

It was his ability to sway people with the spoken word that brought Bryan to Dayton. Already known for his anti-evolution beliefs, he had spoken against Darwinism many times. *The Menace of Darwinism* was published by the Fleming H. Revell Company in 1922. The short book was an extract from Bryan's larger work, *In His Image* by the same publisher, also 1922. In a sense, Bryan had "written the book" on anti-evolution.

Yet, Bryan proved less useful than might have been hoped. While he was a master of stagecraft, he was weak in court proceedings. Fortunately for the state of Tennessee, "General" Tom Stewart, the district's attorney general. (Titles were important to the court with Stewart often called "General," Bryan "Colonel," and, just to keep things balanced, an honorary title of "Colonel" was given to Clarence Darrow.) Bryan had not practiced law in over three decades. He was there in a support role, to deliver the summation for the prosecution and to lend his notoriety to the case.

When Darrow opted out of delivering a summation for Scopes defense and encouraged the court to go ahead and find his client guilty so that they may try the case in a higher court, Bryan lost his moment to shine. And after his disastrous time on the witness stand as an expert witness on the Bible where he took a pounding from Darrow, he needed a second chance to say what he had been prevented from saying earlier.

Robbed of that, he arranged to have editor George Fort Milton of the *Chattanooga News* publish the speech. The address was put in book form by Bryan's publisher that same year.

That speech is important for several reasons. First, it reveals Bryan's motivations for resisting evolution. He harbored concerns that the youth of his day could be and *were* being corrupted by Darwinism. He feared for their spiritual welfare and that of the country.

Second, it dispels, in Bryan's own words, the idea that he hated science, which he did not.

Third, he wanted to show that those who reject Darwin's ideas are neither fools, nor uneducated. He goes to length to show what he perceives are gaps of logic in Darwinism.

Fourth, he feared what was being called "social Darwinism," the idea that the strong should prevail over the weak, and that eugenics is not only logical but good for the human race.

Fifth, that Darwinism steals the soul of every person who adopts its tenets. It was a danger to churches, the Bible, the home, and hope.

Lastly, that evolution will lead to more and worse wars; wars greater than what the country had seen in World War I which took millions of lives.

Agree with Bryan or not, his great concern remained where his interests had always been: the common man.

ABOUT THIS BOOK

THE DEBATES BETWEEN proponents of evolution and those who preach special creation have always been hot and divisive. Charles Darwin published the first of his two major works in November of 1859. *On the Origin of Species* caused a maelstrom that continues to blow today. The release of *The Descent of Man and Selection in Relation to Sex* (1871) only heightened the tension. The topic drew lines and forced people to choose sides. Even churches were divided over the subject with some clergy embracing evolution as God's means of creation while their brethren saw the teaching as the devil's own handiwork.

Evolution was certainly not the only controversy of the 1920s. Debates ranged on many subjects and strained the fabric of the church to the breaking point. Modernism, with its denial of miracles and an inerrant Bible, was being embraced by some church scholars. In response a new and vigorous movement called Fundamentalism arose to challenge what they believed to be heresies.

At stake was control of the subject matter that could be taught in public schools. Did the state have the right to govern teaching the schools they paid for? Or, as Clarence Darrow and others believed, should there be academic freedom in such schools.

Then as now, people align themselves with one side or another of the controversy. Many books and articles have been written about the Scopes trial, both scholarly and popular. The subject matter is such that bias often creeps into the presentation. Such is to be expected. Neutrality is often difficult to maintain. Nonetheless, I have tried to present the following material with no other agenda than to shed light on a famous man's last speech and to sweep away many misguided assumptions about Bryan and his views. This is not to say that everyone will warm to Bryan and his beliefs, but if I've done my work properly then the reader will be able to better understand and articulate Bryan's view of the Scopes trial and the dangers he saw in evolution.

All writers have some bias and I think it only fair to own up to mine. I had several careers before turning to writing. The one career that most pertains to the subject matter of this book is my 22 years as the pastor of Baptist churches. My training and experience makes me sympathetic to Mr. Bryan.

This is not to say that I am unable to see faults. All people have shortcomings. Still, I think Mr. Bryan has been the recipient of bad press. True, in retrospect, he and the others might have done a few things better and avoided doing somethings badly. Still, Mr. Bryan does not deserve the negative comments about his intelligence and motivation. His life is a testimony to creativity, logical thinking, and dedication to the average person. He distinguished himself in Congress, on the campaign trail in three attempts for the office of the presidency, and as secretary of state under President Woodrow Wilson whom he campaigned for. He also showed skill as an editor of a magazine, orator, and proponent of rights for women. His list of accomplishments is long. He was not one to let grass grow under his feet. He remained active until the day he died.

My goal was take the text of a speech meant to be delivered over 90 years ago and illuminate it for those of us far removed from the time and events.

The reader must remember the era in which the trial took place. The thinking, living patterns, education, and the role of government, schools, and the church—especially in the rural south—is different from what we experience today. It should also be remembered that the concept of evolution has changed in some particulars from what was believed in the 1920s.

A word about formatting. I've taken the text as it was published in 1925 (Bryan worked on it until his death. It is, quite literally, his last words on the matter.). I've tried to keep some of the spellings the same as then. The annotations appear in the body of the text which often required splitting paragraphs for easier reading. The text, however, remains unchanged.

There are also a number of notes. Since this work is to be published in print and e-book format, those notes appear as endnotes.

What follows is a chapter on the Scopes Trial to help the reader understand the landscape and history of the event, then follows the annotated text of William Jennings Bryan. The notes are meant to clarify and place in context the points made in the speech—a closing argument that was never delivered.

—Alton Gansky

1925: SCOPES "MONKEY TRIAL"[1]

DAYTON, TENNESSEE WAS a sleepy hamlet of less than 2000 souls. Like many small towns in the South, it had an "Andy of Mayberry" feel. It was not a place for the rich and famous. Instead, hardworking people manned shops or worked the land. Most women felt honored to be called homemakers. Children did there what all children in the rural south did: went to school and did their daily chores.

It is easy to imagine the inviting smells of baking bread or pies coming from the open windows of the homes, of seeing people gather at F. E. Robinson's Rexall pharmacy to chat about the weather, the crops, politics, or news about their ever shrinking town. It was in the pharmacy that a minor conspiracy took place, one that put Dayton on the map and forever fixed its name in the pages of history.

It's been called, "The Trial of the Century." Officially, the case was called *The State of Tennessee v. John Thomas Scopes* but soon became known as the Scopes Monkey Trial. Ninety years later, people are still talking about it. The events of eight days in July 1925 still stir heated opinion.

Historian Jeffery Moran noted, "Nearly 200 journalists from throughout the United States and abroad filed on the order of 135,000 words daily during the trial."[2] Sociologist Howard Odum suggested that if compiled the reports combined work would fill 3000 volumes, each 300 pages long.

It was the first trial to be broadcast over a radio network.

The quiet and sleepy town turned into a circus. So many gathered to watch the proceedings there was no longer room in the courthouse. People stood outside and listened to the goings on through open windows. It became difficult to move around. Nearby, an evangelist hocked his latest book: *Hell and the High School*. Near the end of the trial, Judge John T. Raulston moved the proceedings outside. His reason? He feared the floor of the courtroom would collapse under the weight of the observers.

Interest in the case continued through the decades. Thirty years after the gavel came down for the last time, *Inherit the Wind* by playwrights Jerome Lawrence and Robert Edwin Lee hit the stage. Five years later, in 1960, the movie version played in the nation's theaters. In 2011, the movie *Alleged* took a turn at describing the events of that Tennessee summer.

All of this attention centered not on a major felony but on a misdemeanor. A low level crime. One of the greatest trials in US history revolved around a misdeed that was only slightly more serious than an infraction.

It may be the most important misdemeanor seen in the United States.

The Scopes trial is well-known but little understood. Some imagine it as a legal test between science and religion. It wasn't. While some of that was certainly evident, and while the defense tried to make academic freedom the central issue, the case was, in the strictest terms, a trial about a teacher willfully and knowingly defying state lawmakers. That decision, however, was the perfect tool to bring to light the changing mores of the American people, and others in the Western world.

Changing America

It was the age of Jazz. In the cities, Flapper dresses were the rage. The Roaring Twenties, as they became known, came to stand for fun, frolicking, and immorality. Unlike the previous generation of Gibson Girls who wore their long hair in mounds on their head, sported an hourglass figure, and wore long dresses, Flappers worked hard to be different by looking the same as one another. Boyishness was in for young ladies: severely cropped hair (by that day's standard), short clingy dresses, and bound chests. To much of the country, especially the rural areas, there party lifestyle was puzzling and immoral.

It was the age of F. Scott Fitzgerald whose book *The Great Gatsby*, which came out in the same year as the trial, portrayed the lost generation.

It was the age of transformation. Just two years earlier, World War I ended a conflict that saw the use of tanks, armed airplanes, trench warfare, chlorine gas used as a weapon, and large ship warfare. By the end of the war, the factions had given up nearly ten million dead and over twenty million wounded. The conflict was controversial with many in the US opposing it. The effects of the war reverberated through the country for many years after.

It was the age of science. The Western world was enamored with industrialism, technology and science. In late 1859, Charles Darwin published his first book, *On the Origins of Species*. It would, for a time, be the bible of evolutionary biology and paleontology. Not all scientist of the day agreed with Darwin, but almost all held to some theory of evolution. It would take decades of research and debate before the scientific community came to a consensus. Darwin's second book, *The Descent of Man*, was published in early 1871.

Albert Einstein, in 1922, received the Nobel Prize for his work on the properties of light. Best known for his Special Theory of Relativity and General Theory of Relativity, he had trouble gaining support for the ideas of space-time and bending light. Proving the principles were difficult. Just creating the experiment took time. The British astrophysicist, and devout Quaker, Arthur Eddington proved Einstein right with a series of photographs of a full eclipse. He had traveled halfway around the world to conduct the experiment. The news of his discovery vindicated Einstein and made the physicist world famous.

Science was in the news, society and mores were in flux, and for the first time in US history, more people were living in cities than in the country.

No one would have guessed that tiny, insignificant, rural Dayton, Tennessee would be the center of attention.

The Four Forces of the Twentieth Century Church

WHILE IT IS important to understand the changing face of America in the early 1900s, it is also important to understand the changing shape of the church. Like American society, the church was morphing and not everyone was happy about it. Four forces were shaping the early twentieth century church: modernism, fundamentalism, the holiness movement, and Pentecostalism. Conflict between the first two created the greatest heat.

Modernism was open to change from outside church walls. It could and did tolerate attacks made by liberal scholars ("liberal": as compared to the fundamentalists). They adopted some of the thinking of liberal theologians who challenged basic doctrine, the inerrancy and infallibility of the Bible. This controversy would affect most of the major Protestant denominations and often led to splits.

In 1922, Harry Emerson Fosdick, a liberal Baptist pastor, took a stand against fundamentalism in a sermon delivered in a New York Presbyterian church.

He titled his sermon, "Shall the Fundamentalists Win?" That same year, Fosdick, at the request of the *New York Times*, wrote a rather scathing rebuttal to William Jennings Bryan's article "God and Evolution," which had been published in that same paper on February 26, 1922. Fosdick's piece ran on March 12, 1922.

The controversy between liberal and conservative factions within denominations led to fractures. For example, many conservative Presbyterians split from the denomination to form the Orthodox Presbyterian Church in 1936. Denominations were splitting over matters like the Historical-Critical method of Bible interpretation (often called "Higher Criticism"). The battle continues today.

Fundamentalist held to five statements that served as a test of belief: 1) the inspiration of the Bible by the Holy Spirit and the Bible's inerrancy (that is, the Bible doesn't contain error in the original writings); 2) the reality of Christ's miracles; 3) the virgin birth of Jesus; 4) the belief that Christ atoned (paid the price for our sin and united us with God again) for our sins; and 5) the reality of Christ's physical resurrection. The conservatives in the church battled to keep these doctrines unaltered and untarnished by modernist thinking. They believed the souls of countless people rested in their success.

The Rise of Antievolutionism

IN MANY AREAS of the country, evolution was the popular topic among educated people and the clergy. Evolution, as taught by Darwin and others, did away with God as Creator, and slashed the creation accounts from the Bible. To conservative Christians accepting evolution was the same as denouncing the Bible, at least in part, and if part of the Bible was wrong, how could a person know when it was right?

Little understood among evolutionist was the sacrifice they were demanding church people to make. It wasn't a matter of hating science; it never had been. At the heart of the issue was the validity of the Bible. To dispense with the Bible or even portions of it was to reject the faith they had grown up in, the faith of their fathers and mothers, and be left spiritually twisting in the wind. For those brought up in the Christian faith, the Bible was foundational to life even if they only heard it read from a pulpit. They weren't being asked to modify a belief; they were being summoned to drive a stake through faith's heart.

Less conservative churches and modernists accommodated the new beliefs by suggesting a new approach to interpreting the Bible—an approach that allowed for evolution. Similarly, many evolutionists went out of their way to accommodate the Christians reframing the debate so both sides could be happy. For example, Paul Amos Moody's textbook *Introduction to Evolution* touches on the sensitive nature of the conflict:

As children at home and in their churches they learned about how things started; now at college they hear an entirely different story. This is a really unsettling experience when it involves the book that forms the principal document of our religion. In the light of scientific discoveries must we discard the Bible and with it our religion?

The whole difficulty here lies in the fact that we try to use the Bible in ways for which it was never intended. *It is a book of religion, not a book of science* [italics Moody]. . . . Their (the biblical authors) writing stands or falls on the basis of its worth to religion, not of worth to science."[3]

Scopes' defenders were not so conciliatory. They saw themselves in a battle against self-chosen ignorance, religious bigotry, and the oppression of new ideas. The prosecution worked to enforce a standing law but would also argue for the freedom of the state to dictate what was taught in school—after all, they were the ones who paid for the buildings and teacher salaries.

Political action by antievolutionist did not start in Tennessee. It was the Kentucky General Assembly that, during the winter session of 1921–1922, first attempted to outlaw the teaching of evolution. The bill failed in March of 1922. In the first round of voting the "ayes" and "nays" tied 41–41. The deadlock was broken when legislator Bryce Cundiff cast the needed nay vote. Interestingly, two people who lobbied against the bill were church leaders, including E.Y.

Mullins, president of Southern Baptist Theological Seminary in Louisville.[4]

The razor-edge failure of that bill prompted other states to attempt to do what Kentucky had been unable to achieve. Within two years of the Scopes trial thirteen states considered antievolution bills.

The Tennessee Law

WHERE KENTUCKY HAD failed, Tennessee succeeded. In January 1925, John Washington Butler introduced the Butler Bill. It passed the Tennessee House of Representatives 71–5. It had more trouble making it through the Tennessee Senate, but in March of that year it passed 24–6. Governor Austin Peay signed the bill into law shortly after. Later, in a special address to the legislature, Peay would say, "Nobody believes that it is going to be an active statute."[5] He was wrong.

The bill:

> PUBLIC ACTS OF THE
> STATE OF TENNESSEE
> PASSED BY THE
> SIXTY-FOURTH GENERAL ASSEMBLY
> 1925
>
> CHAPTER NO. 27
> House Bill No. 185
> (By Mr. Butler)

AN ACT prohibiting the teaching of the Evolution Theory in all the Universities, Normals and all other public schools of Tennessee, which are supported in whole or in part by the public school funds of the State, and to provide penalties for the violations thereof.

Section 1. *Be it enacted by the General Assembly of the State of Tennessee*, that it shall be unlawful for any teacher in any of the Universities, Normals and all other public schools of the State which are supported in whole or in part by the public school funds of the State, to teach any theory that denies the story of the Divine Creation of man as taught in the Bible, and to teach instead that man has descended from a lower order of animals.

Section 2. *Be it further enacted*, that any teacher found guilty of the violation of this Act, Shall be guilty of a misdemeanor and upon conviction, shall be fined not less than One Hundred $ (100.00) Dollars nor more than Five Hundred ($500.00) Dollars for each offense.

Section 3. *Be it further enacted*, that this Act take effect from and after its passage, the public welfare requiring it.

Passed March 13, 1925

W. F. Barry, Speaker of the House of Representatives

L. D. Hill, Speaker of the Senate

Approved March 21, 1925.

Austin Peay, Governor.

The body of the bill has less than 200 words in it. Words written by reporters at the trial, and others after the trial surpassed a million words. The Butler Bill would remain the law in Tennessee until 1967.

The Run-Up to the Trial

THE BUTLER BILL met immediate resistance, especially in the North. There was also resistance in the South. Leaders there felt the southern states still suffered from a poor image after the Civil War, and the poverty and trials they endured during Reconstruction only added to post war emotional depression. The "war of northern aggression" was still fresh in southern minds.

Education nationwide was exploding. In 1920 less than one-in-three had a high school education or higher.[6] In the late nineteenth century less than five percent (20,000) of high-school age people attended secondary schools. By 1920 that number exploded to two million, a tenfold increase.[7] Public education was becoming the norm and with it came new issues.

By necessary function, teachers became role models and surrogate parents, at least for a large slice of the day. As school populations grew so did the fear about what was being taught to young minds. Topics such as sex education and patriotism became battlefields. So did the teaching of evolution.

There was a swelling tide of support for freedom of speech in schools and academic freedom (meaning freedom of oversight by those outside the schools and academic leadership). This is no easy issue and continues to be a hot topic. The Scopes trial was less about evolution than about who had the right to decide curriculum.

Enter the American Civil Liberties Union who saw in the Butler Bill similarities to the Espionage Act and The Sedition Act. Created during the days of war, these acts were designed to rid the land of disloyalty. Demanding loyalty oaths from teachers was, to the mind of the ACLU, overreaching and imposed on individual liberties. The Butler Bill wore the same clothing as other efforts to control the schools.

What to do about the anti-evolution bill? To get the Tennessee to overturn it would take years and the election of many new legislators. The best approach was to test the bill in court. On May 4, they ran ads in the major Tennessee newspapers:

> We are looking for a Tennessee teacher who is willing to accept our services in testing this law in the courts. Our lawyers think a friendly test case can be arranged without costing a teacher his or her job.[8]

It was an interesting invitation for business leaders in Dayton to gain publicity. Thirty-one-year-old George W. Rappleyea, a New Yorker who relocated to Dayton—the manager of nearby mines—saw the ad and an idea was born. Rappleyea was an evolutionist and despised the Tennessee law. He attended a Methodist church, one with a minister who saw the

Bible and evolution as compatible. To Rappleyea, this was an opportunity to bring attention to Dayton.

He needed supporters and found them in Frank E. Robinson's drugstore. Robinson was the head of the Rhea County school board, so he was a natural person to approach. Rappleyea pitched his idea of a test case, one that would catch the eye of every state. Robinson liked it. Joining him was School Superintendent Walter White. John Godsey, a local attorney joined the "boosters." Two city attorneys, Herbert and Sue Hicks agreed to prosecute the case. Sue Hicks, Herbert's brother (Sue was named after his mother who died giving birth to him) was, ironically, good friends with the man who would be on trial. Scopes would be tried by a friend. Others would join the effort.

They needed a defendant, a teacher who would agree to teach evolution in violation of the law and stand trial for it. The ACLU would pay all the legal fees (all the attorneys refused payment) and the fine when he was found guilty. Scopes was the perfect pick. Unmarried, boyish, well-liked, Harry Potter glasses perched on this nose, he was pleasant in appearance and demeanor. He was also likely to move out of Dayton sometime in the near future. In another bit of irony, Scopes was not the biology teacher for the school. He taught math, physics, and coached football, but he had been filling in for the principal who normally taught the life science curriculum.

Robinson's pharmacy, like many such stores then and now, did more than dispense medications and fountain drinks; it sold other needed items including books. Scopes, who had met with the "boosters" in the store, retrieved a copy of *Civic Biology* by George William Hunter. The textbook contained a few short sections dealing with evolution. He explained that he had found a copy of the Same book in school storage while he was covering the biology class.

They had their man.

The defense team would grow with the addition of Arthur Garfield Hays who elbowed his way onto the team. He had run against Governor Peay, who had signed the Butler Bill, but lost. He also lost his teaching position and so started his own law school.

The group informed the ACLU and the press. The *Banner* wrote:

> J.T. Scopes, head of the science department of the Rhea County high school, was . . . charged with violating the recently enacted law prohibiting the teaching of evolution in the public schools of Tennessee. Prof. Scopes is being prosecuted by George Rappleyea, manager of the Cumberland Coal and Iron Co., who is represented in the prosecution by S.K. Hicks. The defendant will attack the new law on constitutional grounds. The case is brought as a test of the new law. The prosecution is acting under the auspices of the American Civil Liberties [Union] of New York, which, it is said, has offered to defray the expenses of such litigation.[9]

The Associated Press picked up the story, and soon Dayton, Tennessee was the talk of the nation. There would be another addition to the team that would set the press on fire.

Clarence Darrow

CLARENCE SEWARD DARROW was an enigma. Acerbic, pointed, impatient, willing to resort to name calling in court, he remains the icon for defense attorneys. Once a corporate lawyer, he began to take on lost causes, fighting for those no one else would touch. He fought for labor and for civil rights. There was a fierceness about him and a desire to help the underdog. To many, he is the best defense attorney in US history.

Still, his legal life was not without challenges. Twice he had been accused and tried for jury tampering. He was acquitted in the first case and the second case ended with a hung jury.

He was not afraid to take on the impossible to win cases. In his most famous case, he defended Nathan Leopold, a nineteen-year-old, and Richard Loeb, eighteen, teenagers from wealthy families who had been arrested for killing fourteen-year-old Bobby Franks for the thrill of it. The "boys" as Darrow called them pleaded guilty. This took the case out of the hands of the jury and made it a long sentencing hearing. Darrow's closing remarks lasted twelve hours. In those remarks, he laid out a complicated argument showing Leopold and Loeb were the product of society and—evolution. He succeeded in saving them from execution, but each were sentenced to life plus ninety-nine years in prison.

After the Leopold and Loeb trial, the sixty-eight-year-old Darrow announced his intent to retire. Retirement would not come quickly. He had heard of the Scopes trial but had little interest in it until he learned William Jennings Bryan would be aiding the prosecution. Darrow and Bryan had worked together on political and social issues, but Darrow's opinion of Bryan chilled over time. He considered Bryan too religious for his agnostic blood. He couldn't resist the trial and offered to help the defense team. He wrote:

> In view of the fact that scientists are so much interested in pursuit of knowledge that they cannot make the money that lecturers and Florida real estate agents command, in case you should need us we are willing, without fees or expenses, to help the defense of Professor Scopes.[10]

The ". . . money that lecturers and Florida real estate agents command . . ." crack was aimed at Bryan who made his living speaking, writing, and investing in Florida real estate. The gloves had come off before Darrow had been invited to the fight.

They were happy to have him and the show he would bring with him. The ACLU, however, was less happy. They feared Darrow's rabid anti-religion stance and razor-sharp attacks might do more harm to the cause than good. They had reason to be worried.

Darrow came close to being cited for contempt of court and had to apologize the judge.

In the Scopes trial, Darrow looked like a man who had seen the rough side of life. Stern brow, a hairline in a permanent march away from his forehead, eyes that seemed to read everything written on a person's mind. Photos of him show a dour man who appeared unable to smile. His body had seen sixty-eight years of life, but his mind was sharp and pointed as always. He looked every bit the intimidating, fierce defense attorney. Simply standing to speak could rivet the attention of every person in the courtroom. Without him the Scopes trial might be nothing more than a footnote in Tennessee legal books.

He was a firecracker looking for a flame. The flame had a name: William Jennings Bryan.

Meet the Prosecution

THE PROSECUTION BROUGHT lightening of its own. The number of lawyers on the prosecution caused the defense to complain that their chairs were being stolen. Attorney General Tom Stewart handled most of the court work but all eyes were turned on William Jennings Bryan. A reporter from the Baltimore Sun wrote of Bryan, "He is an old man now but that great body of his still is sturdy as an oak. That barrel chest, the sheer build of man make most of those in the courtroom seem puny and undernourished."[11]

At sixty-five, Bryan still struck an impressive figure and could deliver a speech as good as or better than any man of the day. His "Cross of Gold" message is considered one of the best speeches in US history.[12]

He was a man of some girth with a half-halo of hair around his head. He was quick to smile and quicker with a quip. The 1960 movie *Inherit the Wind*, portrayed him as clownish at times and prone to playing to the audience. (The characters in the movie, although clearly meant to represent the trial participants, all have different names and do not directly represent the real characters.) The movie's characterization is unfair. Bryan had a fine mind and a zeal for public service. He ran for president of the United States three times and served as secretary of state for two years in the Woodrow Wilson administration leaving only after the US entered World War I. He had delivered speeches against the war saying the country would never enter the fray in Europe while he was secretary of state. When the country did, he felt duty-bound to resign.

Bryan was an achiever. He helped bring about the direct election of senators to the upper house of Congress by campaigning for the Seventeenth Amendment which, in 1913, changed the practice of state legislators appointing senators. He also, along with Clarence Darrow, fought for the right of women to vote, a right they were granted in 1920 with the passing of the Nineteenth Amendment. He also fought for prohibition and the Eighteenth Amendment of 1918.

The author of the Butler Bill had consulted Bryan about the measure they were proposing. He supported it but suggested they not levy a fine because it would make martyrs of the teachers. Butler and his supporters ignored the advice and wrote in a minimum fine of $100 and a maximum of $500. While that may not sound like much money, in 1925 the range would be about $1,300 to $6,600. It's a bigger hit than it sounds.

A Media Event, the Media and the Trial

EVERY NEWSPAPER DENOUNCED the trial as a publicity stunt, which, in many ways, it was. No one outside Dayton thought the trial was a good idea. Still, people came in droves. Dayton had the second largest courtroom in the state, but it still was not large enough to hold the growing crowds. It is estimated that over 1,000 people squeezed into the second floor room to watch the proceedings. Coupled with temperatures that hovered around 100 degrees, the courtroom was the least comfortable place in the city.

Dayton had only a few hotels so a committee had been formed to help reporters find lodging in local homes. No one expected this kind of turnout except the "boosters" who orchestrated it all.

The Trial

THE TRIAL WAS overseen by Judge John T. Raulston, a fundamentalist Christian who began each session by having a clergyman lead in prayer, something Darrow would later object to. After threatening to find Darrow in contempt of court, he listened to Darrow's apology, then responded:

> "My friends, and Colonel Darrow, the Man that I believe came into the world to save man from sin, the Man that died on the cross that man might be redeemed, taught that it was godly to forgive and were it not for the forgiving nature of Himself I would fear for man. The Savior died on the cross pleading with God for the men who crucified Him. I believe in that Christ. I believe in these principles. I accept Colonel. Darrow's apology. I am sure his remarks were not premeditated. I am sure that if he had had time to have thought and deliberated he would not have spoken those words. He spoke those words, perhaps, just at a moment when he felt that he had suffered perhaps one of the greatest disappointments of his life when the court had held against him. Taking that view of it, I feel that I am justified in speaking for the people of the great state that I represent when I speak as I do to say to him that we forgive him and we forget it and we commend him to go back home and learn in his heart the words of the Man who said: "If you thirst come unto Me and I will give thee life."[13]

It's difficult to imagine a judge speaking this way from the bench today, and certainly, while Darrow was glad not to be found in contempt, he must have bristled at the overtly Christian message.

The mechanics consisted first of jury selection with Darrow doing most of the questioning. Each was asked if they lived in the area, what they did for work, did they read newspapers and magazines, and if they had read anything about the case or about evolution. A few times Darrow asked if they had heard sermons against evolution. Few had. More shocking, most knew nothing at all about evolution. They had heard of the topic but had never involved themselves in a discussion of the subject.

None of that would matter. While the defense under Darrow fought to have scientists take the stand, they were denied. This became a sore point that illuminates the competing agendas of the legal teams. The Scopes team not only knew they would lose the case, they *wanted* to lose it. A key goal was to take the case to a higher court on appeal where they stood a better chance of getting the Butler Bill declared unconstitutional. Much of their efforts were focused on laying down a case that an appeals court could review and accept. There was no hope or desire to win.

Second, they wanted to use the case to teach the public about evolution and why scientist believed it to be so. They hoped to begin the long process of swaying public opinion. Neither the prosecution nor Judge Raulston were inclined to help them in the process. To them, the trial was a very simple matter: The Tennessee law said no teacher in a publicly funded school could teach that man arose from lower orders of life, or teach anything contrary to the Genesis account of creation. Separation of church state was not as clearly defined as it is in the twenty-first century.

Darrow and his team worked every angle to make the case more about intellectual and academic freedom, about the country's need to embrace current scientific thought about origins and were rebuffed at every turn. The prosecution argued that Scopes knew the law and defied it willfully. There was no requirement for the teacher to embrace the Butler bill but a teacher did have to obey it.

This was something Darrow could not tolerate. He, and many like him, believed in the right of the one; Bryan believed in the right of the majority. If the majority said, "No evolution in the classroom," then there would be no evolution in the classroom. Darrow wanted to protect the individual's right; Bryan wanted to protect the rights of the majority. It was a monumental ideological difference.

Bryan also feared several things about evolution, reasons that made him so set against it. First, he believed the doctrine of evolution could and did serve as an excuse for war. He needed to look back only a few years to World War I for evidence. Second, it took the heart out of political reform, and Bryan was a reformer at heart. Third, Darwinism did away with God and turned the Bible into a book of myths. He was a man of the Bible and wrote a weekly column about the Holy Book. He feared young people of his day were turning away from their spiritual roots. These concerns, as well as others mentioned in what was to be the closing remarks, arose from parents he met on his speaking tours. So many complained that something was happening to their children when they went off to college. These concerns mixed with his belief that employers had certain rights over employees (the opposite of Darrow) and that majority rule was the right way to run society.

Showdown in Dayton, Tennessee

THE ONE EVENT the Scopes trial is remembered for is the showdown between the agnostic Darrow and the Christian Bryan. The tension between the two had continued to grow. Darrow was frustrated with the whole proceedings and had taken to call those who agreed with Bryan "bigots" and "ignoramuses." It was the over the top behavior the ACLU feared.

Darrow did the unthinkable: he called William Jennings Bryan as an expert witness on the Bible. He did this ostensibly to introduce matters for a court of appeals. Bryan, probably unwisely, went against the objection of prosecutor Stewart and picked up Darrow's gauntlet.

Why would he do this? Bryan had not practiced law in thirty years and he must have known that as a witness, he would have to be more careful with his words. Everything he said could be challenged. Darrow treated him as a hostile witness. It turned brutal.

Perhaps Bryan's pride got the best of him. Being in front of crowds is what he did. It was on the podium he was most alive. By his own statements we know he wanted to prove that he was not afraid to be examined by the great atheist. Most of all, he took the stand to defend his faith. Bryan took the stand and the tension escalated.

Darrow's approach was to establish Bryan as a Bible expert. Bryan may have believed himself to be such an expert but the situation called for a biblical apologist, someone trained in the defense of doctrine. Bryan was a great communicator, but he was not properly trained to answer the questions Darrow leveled at him. Interestingly, some of Bryan's answers would put him on the outside of future creationist organizations. For example, he advocated the day-age theory which, while held by many conservative Christians, denies the six, twenty-four hour days of creation in favor of each day representing countless years.

Darrow challenged Bryan on Bishop Ushers 4004 BC date of creation; on the age of the earth; on the Tower of Babel, Buddha; Noah's Flood, Joshua's long day; Jonah; Eve and the Serpent; and more. Bryan makes a valiant effort but must spend much of his time avoiding Darrow's traps. The examination ends abruptly when the judge stops the proceedings for the day.

The next day, Darrow called for a conclusion of the trial claiming they had no evidence or witness they could bring and suggested the court get on with finding John T. Scopes guilty.

Which it did.

The fine was the minimum mandated by law. Another trial was held in an appeals court but the conclusion was the same. The Butler Bill remained on the books until 1967.

Bryan and the State of Tennessee had won the case, but they may have lost the battle.

There were no closing remarks in the Scopes case but both Darrow and Bryan were allowed to make farewell remarks. Bryan said, "The people will determine this issue. They will take sides upon this issue, they will state the question involved in this issue, they will examine the information…"

He was right. The examination, discussion, and debate continues on.

TEXT OF THE SPEECH WITH ANNOTATION

"May it please the Court, and Gentlemen of the Jury:

DEMOSTHENES, (1) THE GREATEST of ancient orators, in his "Oration on the Crown," the most famous of his speeches, began by supplicating the favor of all the gods and goddesses of Greece.

---

(1) Demosthenes (384 BC-322 BC), born in Athens, is known as one of the great Greek orators. He often spoke to power including Philip of Macedonia and Alexander the Great. It is natural that WJB would be drawn to someone known as a master of the spoken word.

If, in a case which involved only his own fame and fate, he felt justified in petitioning the heathen gods of his country, surely we, who deal with the momentous issues involved in this case, may well pray to the Ruler of the Universe for wisdom to guide us in the performance of our several parts in this historic trial. (2) (3)

---

(2) There is some irony here. WJB starts what he considers his most important speech following a formal pattern of rhetoric. His audience is a jury of men only one of whom admitted to having heard anything about evolution. It is unlikely many, if any, would be familiar with Demosthenes. However, he does not dwell on the ancient speaker but on the need to invoke God in the decision the jury was about to make.

(3) WJB's wording, use of emotion, and eloquence might sound strange to the twenty-first century ear, but oratory was still considered an art and a powerful means of bringing about social change. This would decline over the years but WJB maintained that oratory would remain forever: "The age of oratory has not passed; nor will it pass. The press, instead of displacing the orator, has given him a larger audience and enabled him to do more extended work. As long as there are human rights to be defended; as long as there are great interests to be guarded; as long as the welfare of nations is a matter of discussion, so long will public speaking have its place." [14]

Let me, in the first place, congratulate our cause that circumstances have committed the trial to a community like this and entrusted the decision to a jury made up largely of the yeomanry of the State. The book in issue in this trial contains on its first page two pictures contrasting the disturbing noises of a great city with the calm serenity of the country. It is a tribute that rural life has fully earned. (4)

---

(4) The book in question is George William Hunter's *A Civic Biology: Presented in Problems*, (New York: American Book Company, 1914), 2.

I appreciate the sturdy honesty and independence of those who come into daily contact with the earth, who, living near to nature, worship nature's God, and who, dealing with the myriad mysteries of earth and air, seek to learn from revelation about the Bible's wonder-working God. I admire the stern virtues, the vigilance and the patriotism of the class from which the jury is drawn, and am reminded of the lines of Scotland's immortal bard, which, when changed, but slightly, describes your country's confidence in you: (5)

---

(5) A reference to Robert Burns, 1759-1796. The Scopes trial ran from July 10-July 21, 1925. Burns died 129 years before on July 21, 1796. WJB may have had the anniversary of the poet's death in mind when he chose this poem to begin his speech.

O Scotia! my dear, my native soil!
For whom my warmest wish to Heav'n is sent,
Long may thy hardy sons of rustic toil
Be blest with health, and peace, and sweet content!
And oh! may Heav'n their simple lives prevent
From luxury's contagion, weak and vile!
Then howe'er crowns and coronets be rent,
A virtuous populace may rise the while,
And stand a wall of fire around their much-loved isle. (6)

---

(6) "The Cotter's Saturday Night," Robert Burns, stanza 20. The poem contains 21, nine-line stanzas. WJB's speech is divided into 23 subsections. John T. Scopes, quotes a different Burns poem, "To a Louse," 1785, in the preface to his autobiography Center of the Storm, (New York: Holt, Rinehart and Winston, 1967), vi. As to whether this is irony on Scopes' part or just coincidence can't be said with certainty.

Let us now separate the issues from the misrepresentations, intentional or unintentional, that have obscured both the letter and the purpose of the law. This is not an interference with freedom of conscience. A teacher can think as he pleases and worship God as he likes, or refuse to worship God at all. He can believe in the Bible or discard it; he can accept Christ or reject Him. This law places no obligations or restraints upon him. (7)

---

(7) Bryan was a man of "The Book." The Bible was central to his thinking and he applied it to every area of life including politics. In this address he will use "Bible" about 25 times. Defense of the Bible in general and Genesis in particular was one of the reasons he came to Dayton. He came to defend it from the likes of Darrow, modernists, and others he considered a threat to a moral society. It was this adherence to biblical teaching that led to his being called as an expert witness on the Bible (something he denied being.) Denials notwithstanding, Bryan was well known for Bible studies that appeared in some of the nation's newspapers.

And so with freedom of speech, he can, so long as he acts as an individual, say anything he likes on any subject. This law does not violate any rights guaranteed by any Constitution to any individual. (8)

---

(8) Scopes attorneys tried to get the trial moved to federal court and failing that to get the Dayton court to declare the Butler Bill unconstitutional. Bryan attempts to convince the jury that the bill in question does not infringe on freedom of speech or any other constitutional liberty.

It deals with the defendant, not as an individual, but as an employee, official or public servant, paid by the State, and therefore under instructions from the State. (9)

---

(9) WJB addresses the core goal of the trial. Prosecutors were upholding the Butler Bill, Darrow and the defense were doing their best to make the trial about evolution and a teacher's academic freedom to teach such. John Scopes was, in reality, unimportant. In his autobiography he wrote: "At any rate, my own role was a relatively minor one. I furnished the body that was needed to sit in the defendant's chair . . ." [15]

The right of the State to control the public schools is affirmed in the recent decision in the Oregon case, which declares that the State can direct what shall be taught and also forbid the teaching of anything "manifestly inimical to the public welfare."[16] The above decision goes even further and declares that the parent not only has the right to guard the religious welfare of the child but is in duty bound to guard it. That decision fits this case exactly. The State had a right to pass this law and the law represents the determination of the parents to guard the religious welfare of their children.

The Statute Not Conceived in Bigotry

IT NEED HARDLY be added that this law did not have its origin in bigotry. It is not trying to force any form of religion on anybody. The majority is not trying to establish a religion or to teach it—it is trying to protect itself from the effort of an insolent minority to force irreligion upon the children under the guise of teaching science. (10)

---

(10) A reference to the First Amendment and rebuttal to the early statements from the defense that the Butler Bill was unconstitutional.

What right has a little irresponsible oligarchy of self-styled "intellectuals" to demand control of the schools of the United States; in which twenty-five millions of children are being educated at an annual expense of nearly two billion of dollars? (11)

---

(11) This is one of the key points of the prosecutions position. To Clarence Darrow and the defense team, the subject at hand was academic freedom; to WJB and the defense the subject was the State's right to require employees, in this case a teacher, to obey standing laws. To Darrow, et al, a teacher should be allowed to teach his/her own beliefs without limitation; to WJB, et al, the State had a right to require cooperation of the teachers to whom it provided

a salary. Although Darrow and others on Scopes' defense team tried to make the trial about evolution, it never was. (WJB also made evolution a touchstone of the case.) However, it can still be rightly argued that the Butler Bill was as much about evolution as it was the need to control the teaching of the doctrine in public classrooms. The trial, however, focused only on Scopes' flagrant flouting of the law.

Christians must, in every State of the Union build their own colleges in which to teach Christianity; it is duly simple justice that atheists, agnostics and unbelievers should build their own colleges if they want to teach their own religious views or attack the religious views of others.

The statute is brief and free from ambiguity. It prohibits the teaching, in the public schools, of "any theory that denies the story of divine creation as taught in the Bible," and teaches, instead, that man descended from a lower order of animals. The first sentence sets forth the purpose of those who passed the law. They forbid the teaching of any evolutionary theory that, disputes the Bible record of man's creation and, make sure that there shall be no misunderstanding, they place their own interpretation on their language and specifically forbid the teaching of any theory that makes man a descendant of any lower form of life. (12)

(12) Of course, these are the very tenets of evolution. The Butler Bill effectively squashed the teaching of evolution in the public schools of Tennessee.

Evidence Points to the Defendant's Guilt

THE EVIDENCE SHOWS that defendant taught, in his own language as well as from a book outlining the theory, that man descended from lower forms of life. Howard Morgan's testimony gives us a definition of evolution that will become known throughout the world as this case is discussed. (13)

(13) Howard Morgan was a fourteen-year-old student of Scopes. During direct and cross-examination, he maintained that Scopes taught from Lewis Elhuff's *General Science* (Boston: D.C. Heath & Co., 1916). The book does not address human evolution. It appears that young Morgan is relating what Scopes said, not what is contained in Elhuff's book.

Howard, a 14-year-old boy, has translated the words of the teacher and the textbook into language that even a child can understand. As he recollects it, the defendant said: "A little germ of one cell organism was formed in the sea; this kept evolving until it got to be a pretty good sized animal, then came on to be a land animal, and it kept evolving, and from this was man." There is no room for difference of opinion here, and there is no need of expert testimony. Here are the facts, corroborated by another student, Harry Shelton, and admitted to be true by counsel for defense. (14)

---

(14) Harry Shelton was a seventeen-year-old student. The book used at the level was Hunter's 1914 edition of *A Civic Biology*. The book, ironically, had been previously approved for the classroom by the State of Tennessee.

Mr. White, (15) Superintendent of Schools, testified to the use of Hunter's *Civic Biology*,[17] and to the fact that the defendant not only admitted teaching evolution, but declared that he could not teach it without violating the law.

---

(15) Walter White, School Superintendent. He had served as a Republican State Senator "...who liked the antievolution law but loved publicity for his town even more." [Edward J. Larson, *Summer of the Gods* (New York: Basic Books, 1996), 89.]

Mr. Robinson, (16) the Chairman of the School Board, corroborated the testimony of Superintendent White in regard to the defendant's admissions and declarations.

(16) Frank E. Robinson, drugstore owner and chair of the Rhea County school board. One of the primary "conspirators" in setting up the trial case and recruiting John T. Scopes to be the defendant.

These are the facts. They are sufficient and undisputed; a verdict of guilty must follow. (17)

(17) Scopes guilt was never in question. In fact, it was important to the defense that he be found guilty so the case could be tried in a higher court in hopes of having the Butler Bill declared unconstitutional, something that could not be done at the misdemeanor level.

But the importance of this case requires more. The facts and arguments presented to you must not only convince you of the justice of conviction in this case, but, while not necessary to a verdict of guilty, they should convince you of the righteousness of the purpose of the people of the State in the enactment of this law. The State must speak through you to the outside world and repel the aspersions cast by the counsel for the defense upon the intelligence and the enlightenment of the citizens of Tennessee. (18)

(18) The defense team, especially Darrow, were quick to cast aspersions on leaders of Tennessee specifically, Tennesseans in general, and Christians as a whole. For example, in the now famous confrontation between Darrow and WJB, Darrow said, "We have the purpose of preventing bigots and ignoramuses from controlling the education of the United States and you know it ..." (Trial transcripts, p. 299)

The people of this State have a high appreciation of the value of education. The State Constitution testifies to that in its demand that education shall be fostered and that science and literature shall be cherished. (19)

---

(19) WJB references the 1870 Tennessee constitution, which remained unaltered until 1953. Until that year, it was the oldest unamended state constitution. "... it shall be the duty of the general assembly in and future periods of this government, to cherish literature and science." (*Constitution of Tennessee*, Sec. 12, 1870). The line WJB quotes is no longer in the Tennessee constitution.

The continuing and increasing appropriations for public instruction furnish abundant proof that

Tennessee places a just estimate upon the learning that is secured in its schools.

Religion and True Science Do Not Conflict

RELIGION IS NOT hostile to learning; Christianity has been the greatest patron learning has ever had. (20)

---

(20) WJB makes several attempts to show that science is not the issue in this case but the willful breaking of a standing law—valid or not.

But Christians know that "the fear of the Lord is the beginning of wisdom" (21) now just as it has been in the past, and they therefore oppose the teaching of guesses that encourage godlessness among the students. (22)

---

(21) A popular theme in the Bible: Proverbs 1:7, Proverbs 9:10, Psalm 111:10.

(22) WJB, like many in his day, felt that Darwinian evolution had yet to be proven. Indeed, much of what passed for evolutionary science in the 1920s is dismissed out of hand by even the most ardent evolutionists. This is natural of course; the field was young, and several areas of science including dating of fossils, dynamics of

geology, chemistry, and much more were still coming of age.

Neither does Tennessee undervalue the service rendered by science. The Christian men and women of Tennessee know how deeply mankind is indebted to science for benefits conferred by the discovery of the laws of nature and by the designing of machinery for the utilization of these laws. Give science a fact and it is not only invincible, but it is of incalculable service to man. If one is entitled to draw from society in proportion to the service that he renders to society, who is able to estimate the reward earned by those who have given to us the use of steam, the use of electricity and enabled us to utilize the weight of water that flows down the mountainside? Who will estimate the value of the service rendered by those who invented the phonograph, the telephone and the radio? Or, to come more closely to our home life, how shall we recompense those who gave us the sewing machine, the harvester, the threshing machine, the tractor, the automobile and the method now employed in making artificial ice? The department of medicine also opens an unlimited field for invaluable service. Typhoid and yellow fever are not feared as they once were. Diphtheria and pneumonia have been robbed of some of their terrors, and a high place on the scroll of fame still awaits the discovery of remedies for arthritis, (23) cancer, tuberculosis and other dread diseases to which mankind is heir. (24)

(23) WJB's wife Mary Baird Bryan suffered from arthritis much of her adult life and required at times help to stand or to dress. One of the chief reasons they moved to Florida was to ease Mary's pain especially during cold months.

(24) WJB suffered from diabetes, a disease that took his father's life and would, in all probability, contribute to his death less than a week after the trial's end.

Christianity welcomes truth from whatever source it comes and is not afraid that any real truth from any source can interfere with the divine truth that comes by inspiration from God Himself. It is not scientific truth to which Christians object, for true science is classified knowledge, and nothing therefore can be scientific unless it is true. (25)

(25) WJB had an interest and respect for science in general. To help dispel the belief that he was anti-science he, in 1924—just the year before the trial—joined the American Association for the Advancement of Science. This didn't endear him to the science community but it did indicate his belief that science should be respected. His problem with science rested with the growing tendency to dismiss the supernatural, which to WJB meant miracles and the Bible.

Evolution is not Proven

EVOLUTION IS NOT truth; it is merely a hypothesis—it is millions of guesses strung together. (26)

---

(26) This was one of WJB's favorite talking points. He likens a hypothesis to a guess. In a sense he is right, a scientific hypothesis is the beginning of a scientific effort. Observations are made and a hypothesis is suggested. In that sense, a hypothesis is a guess, but in scientific circles it is much more. It begins with observation, moves to speculation, then on to testing. At end of a set of experiments, the hypothesis is revised and the process begins all over. So, Bryan is correct at the foundation of his assumption but does factor in the process and endless rechecking of observation. This riled Presbyterian pastor and theologian Harry Emerson Fosdick who, upon invitation, wrote a piece for the *New York Times* in 1922 ("Evolution and Mr. Bryan," Harry Emerson Fosdick, *New York* Times, March 22, 1922) taking Bryan to task for belittling the term and the process in an article in the same newspaper (February 26, 1922).

It had not been proven in the days of Darwin—he expressed astonishment that with two or three million species it had been impossible to trace any species to any other species—it had not been proven in the days of Huxley (27), and it has not been proven up to today.

---

(27) A reference to Thomas Henry Huxley, "Darwin's Bulldog." Huxley was an English biologist and surgeon. Some attributed the coining of "agnostic" to him as a way of describing his belief. He was a forceful advocate for Darwinism.

It is less than four years ago that Professor Bateson came all the way from London to Canada to tell the American scientists that every effort to trace one species to another had failed—every one. (28)

---

(28) William Bateson (1861-1926) appeared before the American Association for the Advancement of Science. The speech was carried in the 1922 issue of *Science* magazine (January 20, 1922, Vol. LV., page 55) Bateson was an English geneticist, professor at the University of Cambridge, and author. He was an evolutionist. Bryan used this illustration frequently. It appears in his 1922 NYT article (previously mentioned) and in other of his speeches.

He said he still had faith in evolution but had doubts about the origin of species. But of what value is evolution if it cannot explain the origin of species? While many scientists accept evolution as if it were a fact, they all admit, when questioned, that no explanation has been found as to how one species developed into another. (29)

---

(29) It should be remembered that it is 1925. Darwinism is less than seventy years old and while largely accepted in the scientific community, it had yet to become a universal theory among scientists.

Darwin suggested two laws, sexual selection and natural selection. Sexual selection has been laughed out of the class room and natural selection is being abandoned, and no new explanation is satisfactory even to scientists. Some of the more rash advocates of evolution are wont to say that evolution is as firmly established as the law of gravitation (30) or the Copernican theory. (31)

---

(30) A probable reference to a written statement entered into the transcripts although not heard by the jury. The author of the paper was Prof. Horatio Hackett Newman, zoologist, University of Chicago. "The evidences upon which the law of gravity are based are no less indirect than are those supporting the principle of evolution." (Transcript, p. 264)

(31) A reference to defense attorney Arthur Garfield Hays' arguments in which he says, ". . . evolution is as much a scientific fact as the Copernican theory, but the Copernican theory has been fully accepted, as this must be accepted." (Transcripts, p. 57) Hays, named by his father after a series of US presidents, was a successful lawyer who spent much of his time working for the ACLU—of which he was a cofounder—the sponsors of this case.

The absurdity of such a claim is apparent when we remember that anyone can prove the law of gravitation by throwing a weight into the air and that anyone can prove the roundness of the earth by going around it, while no one can prove evolution to be true in any way whatever.

Chemistry is an insurmountable obstacle in the path of evolution. It is one of the greatest of the sciences; it separates the atoms, isolates them and walks about them, so to speak. If there were in nature a progressive force, an eternal urge, Chemistry would find it. But it is not there. All of the ninety-two original elements (32) are separate and distinct; they combine in fixed and permanent proportions.

(32) There are 118 elements on today's periodic table. In WJB's day, the number was 92.

Water is H_2O, as it has been from the beginning. It was here before life appeared (33) and has never changed; neither can it be shown that anything else has materially changed.

---

(33) In WJB thinking and that of other conservative Christians, the unfinished creative state of the Earth prior to the creation week included water: "In the beginning God created the heavens and the earth. The earth was formless and void, and darkness was over the surface of the deep, and the Spirit of God was moving over the surface of the water," (Genesis 1:1-2, NASB).

There is no more reason to believe that man descended from some inferior animal than there is to believe that a stately mansion has descended from a small cottage. Resemblances are not proof—they simply put us on inquiry. As one fact, such as the absence of the accused from the scene of the murder, outweighs all the resemblances that a thousand witnesses could swear to, so the inability of science to trace any one of the millions of species to another species outweighs all the resemblances upon which evolutionists rely to establish man's blood relationship with the brutes.

But while the wisest scientists cannot prove a pushing power, such as evolution is supposed to be, there is a lifting power that any child can understand. 'The plant lifts the mineral up into a higher world, and the animal lifts the plant up into a world still higher. So, it has been reasoned by analogy, man rises, not by a power within him, but only when drawn upward by a higher power. There is a spiritual gravitation that draws all souls toward heaven, just as surely as there is a physical force that draws all matter on the surface of the earth toward the earth's center. Christ is our drawing power; he said. "I, if I be lifted up from the earth, will draw all men unto me," (34) and His promise is being fulfilled daily all over the world. (35)

---

(34) John 12:32 KJV, a well-known passage to churchgoers. The next verse gives context to the passage: "This he said, signifying what death he should die." Jesus was speaking of his death on the cross. "Lifted up" refers to the Roman practice of elevating the crucified on a cross.

(35) It might seem odd to some that WJB would be so overt in his use of Scripture and Christian terms. While it is commonplace in our day to read of protests against Christian symbols on public property or the display of the Ten Commandments in a courtroom, it was commonplace in 1925, especially in the South where church was an integral part of local life to see (as happened in the early days of this trial) a court case begin with prayer. Judge Raulston kept a Bible on his judicial bench. When Raulston threatened Darrow with contempt of court the defense attorney apologized. Raulston

forgave him but only after the judge delivered what amounted to a short sermon on forgiveness. WJB knows his audience and the milieu he is in. By using well-known verses, he is establishing common ground.

It must be remembered that the law under consideration in this case does not prohibit the teaching of evolution up to the line that separates man from the lower form of animal life. The law might well have gone further than it does and prohibit 'the teaching of evolution in lower forms of life; the law is a very conservative statement of the people's opposition to an anti-Biblical hypothesis. The defendant was not content to teach what the law permitted; he, for reasons of his own, persisted in teaching that which was forbidden for reasons entirely satisfactory to the law-makers. (36)

---

(36) WJB is allowing for the possibility of evolution in "lower" forms of life, that is, nonhuman. The issue for him was lowering humans to the level of "lesser" animals. He may have had in mind phrases from the creation account like, "Then God said, 'Let the waters teem with swarms of living creatures, let birds fly above the earth in the open expanse of the heavens'" (Genesis 1:20). Verse 24 is similar. Some theistic evolutionists understand this as evolution

working in the sea on the land. This is much debated among theologians.

Misuses of the Term "Evolution"

MOST OF THE people who believe in evolution do not know what evolution means. One of the science books taught in the Dayton High School has a chapter on the "The Evolution of Machinery." (37)

(37) A reference to Lewis Elhuff's *General Science* mentioned earlier. WJB misspeaks here. The chapter title is "Simple Machines" (p. 175). The first subhead of the chapter is "Evolution of the Machines" (not "Machinery"). This is a minor bit of misspeak. Of course, Elhuff uses the term "evolution" to mean "the development and advancement of."

This is a very common misuse of the term. People speak of the evolution of the telephone, the automobile and the musical instrument. But these are merely illustrations of man's power to deal intelligently with inanimate matter; there is no growth from within in the development of machinery. (38)

(38) "Evolve" comes from the Latin *evolvere* meaning to "roll out of." In the early seventeenth century it came to mean (and continues to mean) "to make

more complex." Today, most use the word in reference to biological development.

Equally improper is the use of the word "evolution" to describe the growth of a plant from a seed, the growth of a chicken from an egg, or the development of any form of animal life from a single cell. All these give us a circle, not a change from one species to another.

Evolution—the evolution in this case, and the only evolution that is a matter of controversy anywhere—is the evolution taught by [the] defendant, set forth in the books now prohibited by the new State law, and illustrated in the diagram printed on page 194 of Hunter's Civic Biology.[18] The author estimates the number of species in the animal kingdom at five hundred and eighteen thousand nine hundred. These are divided into eighteen (39) classes and each class is indicated on the diagram by a circle, proportionate in size to the number of species in each class and attached by a stem to the trunk of the tree.

---

(39) WJB is off by one. Hunter's diagram and list show seventeen categories, not eighteen.

It begins with protozoa and ends with the mammals. Passing over the classes with which the average man is unfamiliar, let me call your attention to a few of the larger and better known groups. The insects are numbered at three hundred and sixty thousand, over two-thirds of the total number of species in the animal world. The fishes are numbered at thirteen thousand, the amphibians at fourteen hundred, the reptiles at thirty-five hundred, and the birds at thirteen thousand, while thirty-five hundred mammals are crowded together in a little circle that is barely higher than the bird circle. No circle is reserved for man alone. He is, according to the diagram, shut up in the little circle entitled "Mammals," with thirty-four hundred and ninety-nine other species of mammals. Does it not seem a little unfair not to distinguish between man and lower forms of life? What shall we say of the intelligence, not to say religion, of those who are so particular to distinguish between fishes and reptiles and birds but put a man with an immortal soul in the same circle with the wolf, the hyena and the skunk? What must be the impression made upon children (40) by such a degradation of man?

---

(40) One of the motivations for WJB was his concern that children would be led away from spiritual belief. He often heard from parents whose children came home from college with their faith in tatters. This is one of the primary reasons he became an anti-evolutionist.

In the preface of this book the author explains that it is for children and adds that "the boy or girl of average ability upon admission to the secondary school is not a thinking individual."[19] Whatever may be said in favor of teaching evolution to adults it surely is not proper to teach it to children who are not yet able to think.

Evolutionist "Proofs" Are Only Guesses. (41)

---

(41) While, technically, the Scopes trial was not about evolution, Darrow's defense team tried to make it so. Consequently, WJB felt compelled to rebut the concept. He often portrayed evolutionary science as a collection of guesses, unsubstantiated by evidence. It was a common view. As mentioned earlier, in 1922, over 3 years before the trial, the *New York Times* (February 26, 1922) ran an article by WJB titled "God and Evolution." He wrote: "The first objection to Darwinism is that it is only a guess and was never anything more. It is called a "hypothesis," but the word 'hypothesis,' though euphonious, dignified and high-sounding, is merely a scientific synonym for the old-fashioned word 'guess.' If Darwin had advanced his views as a guess they would not have survived for a year, but they have floated for half a century, buoyed up by the inflated word 'hypothesis.' When it is understood that 'hypothesis' means 'guess,' people will inspect it more carefully before

accepting it." Edwin Grant Conklin of Princeton University and Henry Fairfield Osborn, president of the American Museum of Natural History responded individually in the NYT on March 5, 1922.

THE EVOLUTIONIST DOES not undertake to tell us how Protozoa, moved by interior and resident forces, sent life up through all the various species, and cannot prove that there was actually any such compelling power at all. And yet the school children are asked to accept their guesses and build a philosophy of life upon them. If it were not so serious a matter, one might be tempted to speculate upon the various degrees of relationship that, according to evolutionists exist between man and other forms of life. It might require some very nice calculation to determine at what degree of relationship the killing of a relative ceases to be murder and the eating of one's kin ceases to be cannibalism.

But it is not a laughing matter when one considers that evolution not only offers no suggestions as to a Creator but tends to put the creative act so far away as to cast doubt upon creation itself. And, while it is shaking faith in God as a beginning, it is also creating doubt as to a heaven at the end of life. Evolutionists do not feel that it is incumbent upon them to show how life began or at what point in their long-drawn-out scheme of changing species man became endowed with hope and promise of immortal life. God may be a matter of indifference to the evolutionists, and a life beyond may have no charm for them, but the mass of mankind will continue to worship their Creator and continue to find comfort in the promise of their Saviour that he has gone to prepare a place for them. Christ has made of death a narrow, star-lit strip between the companionship of yesterday and the reunion of tomorrow; evolution strikes out the stars and deepens the gloom that enshrouds the tomb.

If the results of evolution were unimportant, one might require less proof in support of the hypothesis; but, before accepting a new philosophy of life built upon a materialistic foundation, we have reason to demand something more than guesses: "we may well, suppose" is not a sufficient substitute for "Thus saith the Lord." (42)

---

(42) The phrase, "Thus saith the Lord" appears over 413 times in the Old Testament (Authorized Version) and was used to indicate the prophet's message did not originate with him or with any other human but is a direct message from God. Exodus 4:22 serves as an example: "And thou shalt say unto Pharaoh, Thus saith the LORD, Israel is my son, even my firstborn..."

If you, your honor, and you, gentlemen of the jury, would have an understanding of the sentiment that lies back of the statute against the teaching of evolution, please consider the facts that I shall now present to you. First, as to the animals to which evolutionists would have us trace our ancestry.

Darwin's "Family Tree."

THE FOLLOWING IS Darwin's family tree, as you will find it set forth on pages 180-181 of his *Descent of Man*: (43)

---

(43) WJB uses some of this argument in his book, *In His Image* (New York: Fleming H. Revell Company, 1922), 90.

"The most ancient progenitors in the kingdom of Vertebrata at which we are able to obtain an obscure glance apparently consisted of a group of marine animals resembling the larvae of existing ascidians. These animals probably gave rise to a group of fishes as lowly organized as the lancelot; and from these the Ganoids, and other fishes like the Lepidosiren, must have been duplicated. From such fish a very small advance would carry us on to the amphibians, we have seen that birds and reptiles were once intimately called together, and the Monotremata now connect mammals with reptiles in a slight degree. But no one can at present say by what line of descent the three higher and related classes, namely, mammals, birds and reptiles, were derived from the two lower vertebrata classes, namely, amphibians and fishes. In the class of mammals the steps are not difficult to conceive which led from the ancient Monotremata to the ancient Marsupials: and from these to the early progenitors of the placental mammals. We may thus ascend to the Lemuridae; and the interval is not very wide from these to the Simiadae. The Simiadae then branched off into two great stems, the New World and Old World monkeys; and from the latter, at a remote period, Man, the wonder and glory of the universe, proceeded. Thus we have given to a man a pedigree of prodigious length, but not, it may be said, of noble quality." (Ed. 1874, Hurst.)

Note the words implying uncertainty; "obscure glance," "apparently," "resembling," "must have been," "slight degree" and "conceive."

Darwin, on page 171 of the same book, tries to locate his first man—that is, the first man to come down out of the trees—in Africa. After saving man in company with gorillas and chimpanzees, he says: "But it is useless to speculate on this subject." If he had only thought of this earlier, the world might have been spared much of the speculation that his brute hypothesis has excited.

On page 79 Darwin gives some fanciful reasons for believing that man is more likely to have descended from the chimpanzee than from the gorilla. His speculations are an excellent illustration of the effect that the evolutionary hypothesis has in cultivating the imagination. Professor J. Arthur Thomson (44) says that the "idea of evolution is the most potent thought-economizing formula the world has yet known."[20] It is more than that; it dispenses with thinking entirely and, relies on the imagination.

> (44) Sir John Arthur Thomson (1861-1933) was a Scottish naturalist, Regius professor of natural history at the University of Aberdeen. He authored several books popularizing science. He also wrote *Science and Religion* (1925).

On page 141 Darwin attempts to trace the mind of man back to the mind of lower animals. On pages 113 and 114 he endeavors to trace man's moral nature back to the animals. It is all animal, animal, animal, with never a thought of God or of religion.

Evolution Shakes Faith in Holy Writ

OUR FIRST INDICTMENT (45) against evolution is that it disputes the truth of the Bible account of man's creation and shakes faith in the Bible as the word of God. (46)

> (45) Here begins a five-point series of "indictments" leveled against evolution.
>
> (46) WJB held to a "literal interpretation" of the Bible. Unfortunately, the term is misunderstood by many who lack theological training. When a theologian uses the term "literal" he or she refers to a choice of hermeneutics. Hermeneutics is the organized, systematic study of ancient documents such as the Bible. "Literal" means to take the text in the plain, normal sense of the

> language. When the Bible says God is spirit (John 4:24) it means he has no corporeal body, but when it says God shelters his people under his wings (Psalm 91:4) it does not mean that God has feathers. In other words, one who holds to a literal interpretation of biblical text differentiates between hyperbole, poetics, parable, and historical accounts. WJB, while on the stand and being grilled by Darrow says, "For instance: 'Ye are the salt of the earth.' (Matthew 5:13). I would not insist that man was actually salt, or that he had flesh of salt, but it is used in the sense of salt as saving God's people."

This indictment we prove by comparing the processes described. as evolutionary with the text of *Genesis*. It not only contradicts the Mosaic record as to the beginning of human life, but it disputes the Bible doctrine of reproduction according to kind—the greatest scientific principle known.

Evolution Disputes the Bible's Vital Truth

OUR SECOND INDICTMENT is that the evolutionary hypothesis, carried to its logical conclusion, disputes every vital truth of the Bible. Its tendency, natural, if not inevitable, is to lead those who really accept it, first to agnosticism and then to atheism. Evolutionists attack the truth of the Bible, not openly at first, but by using weasel-words like "poetical," "symbolical" and "allegorical" to suck the meaning out of the inspired (47) record of man's creation. (48) (49)

---

(47) Although not stated as such, this is most likely a reference to modernism. In this context, modernism is the liberal movement in Christian circles, that denied the miraculous, inspiration, and the historical reality of Bible accounts.

(48) WJB uses the word "inspired" in the conservative theological meaning. Taken from the Greek *theopneustos* meaning "God-breathed." The word appears in 2 Timothy 3:16. It carries a greater meaning than someone, like an artist, who is inspired to do something. It is understood in Christian theology to mean that the Bible comes from God and contains everything God wants people to know.

(49) In the opening chapter of *The Last Message of William Jennings Bryan*, George F. Milton, editor of *The Chattanooga News*, relates what he believed to be WJB's last public conversation. Milton received a phone call from WJB regarding the publishing of his undelivered speech. In that conversation he said, "My fight is not with the agnostics or the atheists. I am not engaged in a controversy with them. My fight is with the so-called 'modernists' of the Christian Church over a matter of Christian doctrine and belief, and in this battle I am not concerned with the views of agnostics or infidels." (William Jennings Bryan,

The Last Message of William Jennings Bryan, New York: Fleming H. Revell Company, 1925), 10.

We call as our first witness Charles Darwin. He began life a Christian. On page 39. Vol. I, of the *Life and Letters of Charles Darwin*, by his son, Francis Darwin, he says, speaking of the period from 1828 to 1831: "I did not then in the least doubt the strict and literal truth of every word in the Bible."[21] On Page 412 of Vol. II of the same publication, he says: "When I was collecting facts for the 'Origin' my belief in what is called a personal God was as firm as that of Dr. Pusey (50) himself."[22] It may be a surprise to your honor and to you, gentlemen of the jury, as it was to me, to learn that Darwin spent three years at Cambridge studying for the ministry.

---

(50) Edward Pusey (1800-1882) was an English Anglican minister whose sermon, according to Darwin, challenged Darwin. The sermon was published in the *The Guardian*.

This was Darwin as a young man, before he came under the influence of the doctrine that man came from a lower order of animals. The change wrought in his religious views will be found in a letter written to a German youth in 1879 and printed on Page 277 of vol. 1 of the *Life and Letters* above referred to. The letter begins, "I am much engaged, an old man, and out of health, and I cannot spare time to answer your questions fully,—nor indeed can they be answered. Science has nothing to do with Christ, except in so far as the habit of scientific research makes a man cautious in admitting evidence."[23] For myself, I do not believe that there ever has been any revelation. As for a future life, every man must judge for himself between conflicting vague probabilities."

Note that "science has nothing to do with Christ, (51) except in so far as the habit of scientific research makes a man cautious in admitting evidence."

---

(51) WJB used this material in his *In His Image.* William Jennings Bryan, *In His Image*, (New York: Fleming H. Revell Company, 1922), 113, 114.

Stated plainly, that simply means that "the habit of scientific research" makes one cautious in accepting the only evidence that we have of Christ's existence, mission, teachings, crucifixion and resurrection, namely the evidence found in the Bible. To make this interpretation of his words the only possible one, he adds "for myself, I do not believe that there ever has been any revelation," in rejecting the Bible as a revelation from God, he rejects the Bible's conception of God, and he rejects also the supernatural Christ of whom the Bible, and the Bible alone, tells. And, it will be observed, he refuses to express any opinion as to a future life.

What His Hypothesis Did for Darwin

NOW LET US follow with his son's exposition of his father's views as they are given in extracts from a biography written in 1876. Here is Darwin's language as quoted by his son:

> "During these months (October, 1838, to January, 1839) I was led to think much about religion. Whilst on board the *Beagle* I was quite orthodox, and I remember being heartily laughed at by several of the officers (though themselves orthodox) for quoting the Bible as an unanswerable authority on some point of morality. When thus reflecting, I felt compelled to look for a First Cause, having an intelligent mind in some degrees analogous to man: and I deserved to be called an atheist. This conclusion was strong in my mind, about the time, as far as I can remember when I wrote the *Origin of Species*; it is since that time that it has very gradually, with many fluctuations, become weaker. But then arises the doubt, Can the mind of man, which has, as I fully believe, been developed from a mind as low as that possessed by the lowest animals, be trusted when it draws such grand conclusions?"[24]
>
> "I cannot pretend to throw the least light on such abstruse problems. The mystery of the beginning of all things is insoluble by us; and I for one must be content to remain an agnostic."[25]

When Darwin entered upon his scientific career he was "quite orthodox and quoted the Bible as an unanswerable authority on some point or morality:" Even when he wrote the *Origin of Species*, the thought of "a First Cause, having an intelligent mind in some degree analogous to man" was strong in his mind. It was after that time that "very gradually, with many fluctuations," his belief in God became weaker. He traces this decline for us and concludes by telling us that he cannot pretend to throw the least light on such abstruse problems—the religious problems above referred to. Then comes the flat statement that he "must be content to remain an agnostic"; and to make clear what he means by the word agnostic. he says that "the mystery of the beginning of all things is insoluble by us"—not by him alone but by everybody. Here we have the effect of evolution upon its most distinguished exponent; it led him from an orthodox Christian, believing every word of the Bible and in a-personal God, down and down and down to helpless and hopeless agnosticism.

But there is one sentence upon which I reserved comment—it throws light upon his downward pathway. "Then arises the doubt, can the mind of man, which has, as I fully believe, been developed from a mind as low as that possessed by the lowest animals, be trusted when it draws such grand conclusions?"[26]

Here is the explanation: He drags man down to the brute level, and then, judging man by brute standards, he questions whether man's mind can be trusted to deal with God and immortality!

How can any teacher tell his students that evolution does not tend to destroy his religious faith? How can an honest teacher conceal from his students the effect of evolution upon Darwin himself? And is it not stranger still that preachers who advocate evolution never speak of Darwin's loss of faith, due to his belief in evolution? The parents of Tennessee have reason enough to fear the effect of evolution on the minds of their children. Belief in evolution cannot bring to those who hold such a belief any compensation for the loss of faith in God, trust in the Bible, and belief in the supernatural character of Christ. It is belief in evolution that has caused so many scientists and so many Christians to reject the miracles of the Bible, and then give up, one after another, every vital truth of Christianity. They finally cease to pray and sunder the tie that binds them to their Heavenly Father.

Miracles Possible with God

A MIRACLE SHOULD not be a stumbling block to anyone. (52)

---

(52) The most dramatic sequence of the Scopes trial took place when WJB agreed to be questioned by Darrow. During the exchange, Darrow made several attempts to dismiss the miracles of the Bible. WJB did his best, as much as someone in

a witness stand can, to defend the historical accuracy of biblical miracles.

It raises but three questions:

First: Could God perform a miracle? Yes, the God who created the universe can do anything He wants to with it. He can temporarily suspend any law that he has made or he may employ higher laws that we do not understand.

Second: Would God perform a miracle? To answer that question in the negative one would have to know more about God's plans and purposes than a finite mind can know, and yet some are so wedded to evolution that they deny that God would perform a miracle merely because a miracle is inconsistent with evolution.

If we believe that God can perform a miracle and might desire to do so, we are prepared to consider with open mind the third question, namely—did God perform the miracles recorded in the Bible? The same evidence that establishes the authority of the Bible establishes the truth of the record of miracles performed.

Now let me read to the honorable court and to you, gentlemen of the jury, one of the most pathetic confessions that has come to my notice. George John Romanes, (53) a distinguished biologist, sometimes called the successor of Darwin, was prominent enough to be given extended space in both the *Encyclopedia Britannica* and the *Encyclopedia Americana*.

(53) George John Romanes (1848-1894) was a Canadian-born biologist and proponent of comparative psychology, the study of animal behavior. He coined the term "neo-Darwinism." He died at the age of 46.

Like Darwin, he was reared in the orthodox faith, and like Darwin, was led away from it by evolution (see *Thoughts on Religion*, page 180).[27] For twenty-five years he could not pray. Soon after he became an agnostic, he wrote a book entitled, *A Candid Explanation of Theism*, publishing it under an assumed name, "Physicus." In this book (see page 29, *Thoughts on Religion*), he says:

> "And forasmuch as I am far from being able to agree with those who affirm that the twilight doctrine of the 'new faith' is a desirable substitute for the waning splendor of 'the old,' I am not ashamed to confess that with this virtual negation of God the universe to me has lost its soul of loveliness; and although from henceforth the precept to 'work while it is day' will doubtless but gain an intensified force from the terribly intensified meaning of the words that 'the night cometh when no man can work,' yet when at times I think, as think at times I must, of the appalling contrast between the hallowed glory of that creed which once was mine, and the lonely mystery of existence as now I find it—at such times I shall ever feel it impossible to avoid the sharpest pang of which my nature is susceptible."[28]

Do these evolutionists stop to think of the crime they commit when they take faith out of the hearts of men and women and lead them out into a starless night? What pleasure can they find in robbing a human being of "the hallowed glory of that creed" that Romanes once cherished, and in substituting "the lonely mystery of existence" as he found it? Can the fathers and mothers of Tennessee be blamed for trying to protect their children from such a tragedy?

If anyone has been led to complain of the severity of the punishment that hangs over the defendant, let him compare this crime and its mild punishment, (54) with the crimes for which a greater punishment is prescribed.

---

(54) After less than ten minutes of jury deliberation, John T. Scopes was found guilty of a misdemeanor and ordered to pay a fine of $100 (about $1200 in today's money). The verdict was appealed to the Supreme Court of Tennessee (*Scopes v. State*, 154 Tenn. 105, 1927).

What is the taking of a few dollars from one in day or night in comparison with the crime of leading one away from God and away from Christ? (55)

---

(55) To understand WJB's zeal one must understand the conservative Christian doctrine of life after

death. In WJB's world, faith was not a matter of doing good and feeling loved by God. A person's eternity rested with the acceptance or rejection of Christ. Conservative doctrine teaches that everyone continues to live after death, that a future resurrection comes to everyone—some to eternal life; the others to eternal punishment. WJB is concerned with what people, children especially, believed because that belief dictated their eternal future. To WJB, evolutionists were not just teaching some strange doctrine but they were dragging people to Hell with the teaching. For him it was a struggle between eternal life and eternal punishment.

"Offending the Little Ones"

SHAKESPEARE REGARDS THE robbing one of his good name as much more grave than the stealing of his purse. (56)

---

(56) From Othello, Act 3, scene 3, 155-161:
"Good name in man and woman, dear my lord,
Is the immediate jewel of their souls.
Who steals my purse steals trash; 'tis something, nothing; 'Twas mine, 'tis his, and has been slave to thousands; But he that filches from me my good name robs me of that which not enriches him, and makes me poor indeed."

And makes me poor indeed.

But we have a higher authority than Shakespeare to invoke in this connection. He who spake as never man spake thus describes the crimes that are committed against the young: "It is impossible but that offenses will come; but woe unto him through whom they come. It were better for him that a millstone were hanged about his neck, and be cast into the sea, than that he should offend one of these little ones."[29]

Christ did not overdraw the picture. Who is able to set a price upon the life of a child—a child into whom a mother has poured her life and for whom a father has labored? What may a noble life mean to the child itself, to the parents and to the world?

And it must be remembered that we can measure the effect on only that part of life which is spent on earth; we have no way of calculating the effect on that infinite circle of life of which existence here is but a small arc. The soul is immortal and religion deals with the soul; the logical effect of the evolutionary hypothesis is to undermine religion and thus affect the soul. I recently received a list of questions that were to be discussed in a prominent Eastern school for women. The second question in the list read "is religion an obsolescent function that should be allowed to atrophy quietly without arousing the passionate prejudice of outworn superstition?" The real attack of evolution, it will be seen, is not upon orthodox Christianity, or even upon Christianity, but upon religion—the most basic fact in man's existence and the most practical thing in life.

"Higher" culture and Unbelief

BUT I HAVE some more evidence of the effect of evolution upon the life of those who accept it and try to harmonize their thought with it.

James H. Leuba, a professor of psychology at Bryn Mawr College, Pennsylvania, published a few years ago a book entitled *Belief in God and Immortality.* (57)

---

(57) American James H. Leuba (1867-1946) was a psychologist whose views of religion fit best in naturalism, the belief that only natural laws (not supernatural activities) can operate in the world.

In this book he relates how he secured the opinions of scientists as to the existence of a personal God and a personal immortality. He used a volume entitled *American Men of Science*,[30] which he says included the names of "practically every American who may properly be called a scientist."[31] There were fifty-five hundred names in the book. He selected one thousand names as representative of the fifty-five hundred and addressed them personally. Most of them, he said, were teachers in schools of higher learning. The names were kept confidential. Upon the answers received, he asserts that over half of them doubt or deny the existence of a personal God and a personal immortality, and he asserts that unbelief increases in proportion to prominence, the percentage of unbelief being greatest among the most prominent. Among biologists, believers in a personal God numbered less than thirty-one per cent, while believers in a personal immortality numbered only thirty-seven per cent.

He also questioned the students in nine colleges of high rank and from one thousand answers received, ninety-seven per cent of which were from students between eighteen and twenty, he found that unbelief increased from eighteen percent. In the freshman class up to forty to forty-five per cent among the men who graduated. On page 280 of this book we read: "The students' statistics show that young people enter college possessed of the beliefs still accepted, more or less perfunctorily, in the average home of the land, and gradually abandon the cardinal Christian beliefs."[32] This change from belief to unbelief he attributes to the influence of the persons "of high culture under whom they studied."[33]

The people of Tennessee have been patient enough; they acted none too soon. How can they expect to protect society, and even the Church, from the deadening influence of agnosticism and atheism if they permit the teachers employed by taxation to poison the minds of the youth with this destructive doctrine? (58)

---

(58) WJB raises the real issue of the case again, which is: What is the state to do with a teacher who draws a salary from local and state monies but knowingly defies a state statue forbidding the teaching of some topic?

And remember that the law has not heretofore required the writing of the word "poison" on poisonous doctrines. The bodies of our people are so valuable that druggists and physicians must be careful to properly label all poisons. Why not be as careful to protect the spiritual life of our people from the poisons that kill the soul?

There is a test that is sometimes used to ascertain whether one suspected of mental infirmity is really insane. He is put into a tank of water and told to dip the tank dry while a stream of water flows into the tank. If he has not sense enough to turn off the water, he is adjudged insane. Can parents justify themselves if, knowing the effect of belief in evolution, they permit irreligious teachers to inject skepticism and infidelity in the minds of their children?

The Effect of Bad Doctrine

DO BAD DOCTRINES corrupt the morals of students? We have a case in point, Mr. Darrow, one of the most distinguished criminal lawyers in our land, was engaged about a year ago in defending two rich men's sons who were on trial for as dastardly a murder as was ever committed. The older one, "Babe" Leopold, (59) was a brilliant student, nineteen years old. He was an evolutionist and an atheist. He was also a follower of Nietzsche, whose books he had devoured and whose philosophy he had adopted. Mr. Darrow made a plea for him, based upon the influence that

Nietzsche's (60) philosophy had exerted upon the boy's mind. Here are extracts from his speech:

---

(59) Richard Loeb and Nathan "Babe" Leopold were teenagers who beat fourteen-year-old Robert Franks to death in Chicago in 1924. Both were convicted. Darrow was retained by the boy's parents to help with the defense and to keep the two from the death penalty. Darrow's summation lasted twelve hours. Leopold and Loeb were both sentenced to life in prison plus ninety-nine years. Leopold was released on parole in 1958. He died of a heart attack in Puerto Rico at the age of 66. Loeb was killed by another inmate in prison. He was thirty years old.

(60) Friedrich Nietzsche (1844-1900) was a German philosopher who also was a poet, composer, and ancient language scholar. He was a noted atheist.

"Babe took to philosophy.... He grew up in this way; he became enamored by the philosophy of Nietzsche. Your honor, I have read almost everything that Nietzsche ever wrote. A man of wonderful intellect; the most original philosopher of the last century. A man who made a deeper imprint in philosophy than any other man within a hundred years, whether right or wrong. More books have been written about him than probably all the rest of the philosophers in a hundred years. More college professors have talked about him. In a way, he has reached more people, and still he has been a philosopher of what we might call the intellectual cult.

"He wrote one book called *Beyond the Good and Evil*, (61) which was a criticism of all moral precepts, as we understand them, and a treatise that the intelligent man was beyond good and evil, that the laws for good and the laws for evil did not apply to anybody who approached the superman.

---

(61) The book was originally published in German as *Jenseits von Gut und Böse* (1886).

He wrote on the will to power.

"I have just made a few short extracts from Nietzsche that show the things that he [Leopold] has read, and these are short and almost taken at random. It is not how this would affect you. It is not how it would affect me. The question is, how it would affect the impressionable, visionary, dreamy mind of a boy—a boy who should never have seen it—too early for him.

"Here is what Nietzsche says: 'Why so soft, oh, my brethren? Why so soft, so unresisting and yielding? Why is there so much disavowal and abnegation in your heart? Why is there so little fate in your looks? For all creators are hard, and it must seem blessedness unto you to press your hand upon millenniums and upon wax. This new table, oh, my brethren, I put over you; become hard. To be obsessed by moral consideration presupposes a very low grade of intellect. We should substitute for morality the will to our own end, and consequently to the means to accomplish that. A great man, a man whom nature has built up and invented in a grand style, is colder, harder, less cautious and more free from the fear of public opinion. He does not possess the virtues which are compatible with respectability, with being respected, nor any of those things which are counted among the virtues of the herd."

"The superman, a creation of Nietzsche, has permeated every college and university in the civilized world. There is not any university in the world where the professor is not familiar with Nietzsche, not one. . . . Some believe it and some do not believe it. Some read it as I do and take it as a theory, a dream, a vision, mixed with good and bad, but not in any way related to human life. Some take it seriously. . . . There is not a university in the world of any high standing where the professors do not tell you about Nietzsche and discuss him, or where the books are not there.

"If this boy is to blame for this, where did he get it? Is there any blame attached because somebody took Nietzsche's philosophy seriously and fashioned his life upon it? And there is no question in this case but what that is true. Then who is to blame? 'The university would be more to blame than he is; the scholars of the world would be more to blame than he is. The publishers of the words . . . are more to blame than he is. Your Honor, it is hardly fair to hang a 19-year-old boy for the philosophy that was taught him at the university. It does not meet my ideas of justice and fairness to visit upon his head the philosophy that has been taught by university men for twenty-five years."

In fairness to Mr. Darrow, I think I ought to quote two more paragraphs. After this bold attempt to excuse the student on the ground that he was transformed from a well-meaning youth into a murderer by the philosophy of an atheist, and on the further ground that this philosophy was in the libraries of all the colleges and discussed by the professors—some adopting the philosophy and some rejecting it—on these two grounds he denies that the boy should be held responsible for the taking of human life. He charges that the scholars in the universities were more responsible than the boy, and that the universities were more responsible than the boy, because they furnished such books to the students, and then he proceeds, to exonerate the universities and the scholars, leaving nobody responsible. Here is Mr. Darrow's language:

"Now, I do not want to be misunderstood about this. Even for the sake of saving the lives of my clients, I do not want to be dishonest and tell the court something that I do not honestly think in this case. I do not think that the universities are to blame. I do not think they should be held responsible. I do think, however, that they are too large, and that they should keep a closer watch, if possible, upon the individual.

"But you cannot destroy thought because, forsooth, some brain may be deranged by thought. It is the duty of the university, as I conceive it, to be the greatest storehouse of the wisdom of the ages, and to have its students come there and learn and choose. I have no doubt but what it has meant the death of many, but that we cannot help."

A Sinister Flower

THIS IS A DAMNABLE philosophy, and yet it is the flower that blooms on the stalk of evolution. Mr. Darrow thinks the universities are in duty bound to feed out this poisonous stuff to their students, and when the students become stupefied by it and commit murder neither they nor the universities are to blame. I am sure, your Honor, and gentlemen of the jury, that you agree with me when I protest against the adoption of any such a philosophy in the State of Tennessee. A criminal is not relieved from responsibility merely because he found Nietzsche's philosophy in a library which ought not to contain it. Neither is the university guiltless if it permits such corrupting nourishment to be fed to the souls that are entrusted to its care. But go a step further: Would the State be blameless if it permitted the universities under its control to be turned into training schools for murderers? When you get back to the root of this question, you will find that the Legislature not only had a right to protect the students from the evolutionary hypothesis, but was in duty bound to do so.

While on this subject, let me call your attention to another proposition embodied in Mr. Darrow's speech. He said that Dicky Loeb, the younger boy, had read trashy novels of the blood and thunder sort. He even went so far as to commend an Illinois statute which forbids minors reading stories of crime. Here is what Mr. Darrow said:

"We have a statute in this State, passed only last year, if I recall it, which forbids, minors reading stories of crime. Why? There is only one reason; because the Legislature in its wisdom thought it would have a tendency to produce these thoughts and this life in the boys who read them."

If Illinois can protect her boys, why cannot this State protect the boys of Tennessee? Are the boys of Illinois any more precious than yours?

But to return to the philosophy of an evolutionist. Mr. Darrow said: "I say to you seriously that the parents of Dicky Loeb are more responsible than he, and yet few boys had better parents." . . . Again he says: "I know that one of two things happened to this boy; that this terrible crime was inherent in his organism and came from some ancestor, or that it came through his education and his training after he was born." He thinks the boy was not responsible for anything; his guilt was due, according to this philosophy, either to heredity or environment.

But let me complete Mr. Darrow's philosophy based on evolution. He says "I do not know what remote ancestor may have sent down the seed that corrupted him, and I do not know through how many ancestors it may have passed until it reached Dicky Loeb. All I know is, it is true, and there is not a biologist in the world who will not say I am right."

Psychologists who build upon the evolutionary hypothesis teach that man is nothing but a bundle of characteristics inherited from brute ancestors. That is the philosophy which Mr. Darrow applied in this celebrated criminal case. "Some remote ancestor"—he does not know how remote— "sent down the seed that corrupted him." You cannot punish the ancestor—he is not only dead but, according to the evolutionists, he was a brute and may have lived a million years ago. And he says that all the biologists agree with him—no wonder so small a proportion of the biologists, according to Leuba, believe in a personal God.

This is the quintessence of evolution, distilled for us by one who follows that doctrine to its logical conclusion. Analyze this dogma of darkness and death. Evolutionists say that back in the twilight of life a beast, name and nature unknown, planted a murderous seed and that the impulse that originated in that seed throbs forever in the blood of the brute's descendants, inspiring killings innumerable, for which murderers are not responsible because coerced by a fate fixed by the laws of heredity. It is an insult to reason and shocks the heart. That doctrine is as deadly as leprosy; it may aid a lawyer in a criminal case, but it would, if generally adopted, destroy all sense of responsibility and menace the morals of the world. (62)

---

(62) This line of thinking shows one of the things that WJB feared the most. Evolution, to him, was not a scientific theory, but a corrosive agent to morals and peaceful behavior. WJB felt a wide adoption of Darwinism would lead to further wars (something he will address in this speech) and,

> instead of creating an enlightened civilization, would instead free people to be as violent and as cruel as they choose and provide a defense for lawless activity: "We are only acting according to the nature we received from our ancestors. Where Darrow and others saw evolution as an advancement of scientific thinking, WJB saw it as the erosion of human law and peaceful coexistence among neighbors and nations.

A brute, they say, can predestine a man to crime, and yet they deny that God incarnate in the flesh can release a human being from this bondage or save him from ancestral sins. No more repulsive doctrine was ever proclaimed by man. If all the biologists of the world teach this doctrine—as Mr. Darrow says they do—then may heaven defend the youth of our land from their impious babblings.

Evolution Promotes Trifling Speculation

OUR THIRD INDICTMENT against evolution is that it diverts attention from pressing problems of great importance to trifling speculation. While one evolutionist is trying to imagine what happened in the dim past, another is trying to pry open the door of the distant future. One recently grew eloquent over ancient worms and another predicted that seventy-five thousand years hence everyone will be bald and toothless. Both those who endeavor to clothe our remote ancestors with hair and those who endeavor to remove the hair from the heads of our remote descendants (63) ignore the present, with its imperative demands.

---

(63) A study of WJB's speaking shows he often used humor to drive home a point. This is something he had in common with Darrow, who often went for a laugh if it would make his point clearer. WJB was expert in the use of turn of phrase. This remains a technique of polemics today.

The science of "How to Live" is the most important of all the sciences. It is desirable to know the physical sciences, but it is necessary to know how to live. Christians desire that their children shall be taught all the sciences, but they do not want them to lose sight of the Rock of Ages (64) while they study the age of the rocks; neither do they desire them to become so absorbed in measuring the distance between the stars that they will forget Him who holds the stars in His hand. (65)

---

(64) A reference to Christ and a reference to a popular and enduring hymn by Augustus Montague Toplady (1763) still sung in churches today.

(65) A reference to the omnipotence and transcendence of God. WJB might have had

Revelation 1:16 in mind: "And he had in his right hand seven stars..."

While not more than two per cent (66) of our population are college graduates, these, because of enlarged powers, need a "heavenly vision" even more than those less learned, both for their own restraint and to assure society that their enlarged powers will be used for the benefit of society and not against the public welfare.

---

(66) By the time of the Scopes trial, education had become a hot topic in homes across the nation. At the turn of the twentieth century, less than five per cent of high-school-age students attended secondary schools. Now with WWI over, attendance began to climb. Close to two million students attended high school by 1920. With that growth came a wider range of topics, topics many parents of the time found uncomfortable: sex education and evolution being just two. The note WJB sounds here resonated with many parents and certainly would hit home with a jury drawn from a small, rural town.

Evolution is deadening the spiritual life of a multitude of students. Christians do not desire less education, but they desire that religion shall be entwined with learning so that our boys and girls will return from college with their hearts aflame with love of God and love of fellowmen, and prepared to lead in the altruistic work that the world so sorely needs. The cry in the business world, in the industrial world, in the professional world, in the political world—even in the religious world—is for consecrated talents—for ability plus a passion for service. (67)

---

(67) This line, easy as it is to overlook, highlights the differences in social philosophy between WJB and Darrow. Darrow felt strongly about individual rights over societies rights, as did the ACLU. WJB saw the needs of society as more important than the needs of the individual.

Evolution Chills Enthusiasm

OUR FOURTH INDICTMENT against the evolutionary hypothesis is that, by paralyzing the hope of reform, it discourages those who labor for the improvement of man's condition. Every upward-looking man or woman seeks to lift the level upon which mankind stands, and they trust that they will see beneficent changes during the brief span of their own lives. Evolution chills their enthusiasm by substituting aeons for years. It obscures all beginnings in the mists of endless ages. It is represented as a cold and heartless process, beginning with time and ending in eternity, and acting so slowly that even the rocks cannot preserve a record of the imaginary changes through which it is credited with having carried an original germ of life that appeared some time from somewhere. Its only program for man is scientific breeding, a system under which a few supposedly superior intellects, self-appointed, would direct the mating and the movements of the mass of mankind—an impossible system. Evolution, disputing the miracle, and ignoring the spiritual in life, has no place for the regeneration of the individual. It recognizes no cry of repentance and scoffs at the doctrine that one can be born again.

It is thus the intolerant and unrelenting enemy of the only process that can redeem society through the redemption of the individual. An evolutionist would never write such a story as "The Prodigal Son"; (68) it contradicts the whole theory of evolution.

---

(68) WJB references Luke 15:11-31. The Prodigal Son is one of Jesus' best known parables. It is also known as The Parable of the Lost Son. A parable is an ancient teaching technique and often used by Jesus. It is a simple story used to teach a spiritual lesson. In evangelical circles it is often described as an earthly story with a heavenly meaning. Thirty-three parables appear in the synoptic Gospels (the first three Gospels). Those in the jury would recognize the reference immediately.

The two sons inherited from the same parents and, through their parents, from the same ancestors, proximate and remote. And these sons were reared at the same fireside and were surrounded by the same environment during all the days of their youth, and yet they were different. If Mr. Darrow is correct in the theory applied to Loeb, namely, that his crime was due either to inheritance or to environment, how will he explain the difference between the elder brother and the wayward son? The evolutionist may understand from observation, if not by experience, even though he cannot explain, why one of these boys was guilty of every immorality, squandered the money that the father had laboriously earned and brought disgrace upon the family name; but his theory does not explain why a wicked young man underwent a change of heart, confessed his sin, and begged for forgiveness. And because the evolutionists cannot understand this fact, one of the most important in the human life, he cannot understand the infinite love of the heavenly father who stands ready to welcome home any repentant sinner, no matter how far he has wandered, how often he has fallen, or how deep he has sunk in sin.

Your honor has quoted from a wonderful poem, written by a great Tennessee poet, Walter Malone. (69)

---

(69) On the seventh day of the trial, Judge Ralston quoted the third stanza of Walter Malone's poem "Opportunity" when forgiving Clarence Darrow for his misbehavior in the courtroom. Darrow had

apologized but had to endure a spiritual lecture from the fundamentalist judge. "Dost thou behold thy lost youth, all aghast, / Dost thou reel from retribution's righteous blow / Then turn from the blotted archives of the past / And find the future pages white as snow. / Art thou a mourner? Rouse thee from thy spell; / Art thou a sinner? Sin may be forgiven. / Each day gives thee light to lead thy feet from hell. / Each night a star to lead thy feet to heaven." (Walter Malone, 1866-1915, public domain.)

I venture to quote another stanza which puts into exquisite language the new opportunity which a merciful God gives to every one who will turn from sin to righteousness:

Though deep in mire, wring not your hands and weep:
I lend my arm to all who say. "I can." No shame-faced outcast ever sank so deep.
But he might rise and be again a man. (70)

---

(70) Walter Malone, (1866-1915), lawyer, judge, poet. WJB quotes the final stanza. By quoting from the same poem, WJB may be courting favor with Judge Ralston and by mentioning the Tennessee poet may be firming up common ground.

There are no lines like these in all that evolutionists have ever written. Darwin says that science has nothing to do with the Christ who taught the spirit embodied in the words of Walter Malone, and yet this spirit is the only hope of human progress. A heart can be changed in the twinkling of an eye and a change in the life follows a change in the heart. If one heart can be changed, it is possible that many hearts can be changed, and if many hearts can be changed it is possible that all hearts can be changed—that a world can be born in a day. It is this fact that inspires all who labor for man's betterment. It is because Christians believe in individual regeneration and in the regeneration of society through the regeneration of individuals that they pray. "Thy kingdom come, Thy will be done on earth as it is in heaven."[34] Evolution makes a mockery of the Lord's Prayer!

To interpret the words to mean that the improvement desired must come slowly through unfolding ages,—a process with which each generation could have little to do—is to defer hope, and hope deferred maketh the heart sick.

Evolution Would Eliminate Love

OUR FIFTH INDICTMENT of the evolutionary hypothesis is that, if taken seriously and made the basis of a philosophy of life, it would eliminate love and carry man back to a struggle of tooth and claw. The Christians who have allowed themselves to be deceived into believing that evolution is a beneficent, or even a rational process have been associating with those who either do not understand its implications or dare not avow their knowledge of these implications. Let me give you some authority on this subject. I will begin with Darwin, the high priest of evolution, to whom all evolutionists bow.

On pages 149 and 150, in *The Descent of Man*,[35] already referred to, he says:

> "With savages, the weak in body or mind are soon eliminated; and those that survive commonly exhibit a vigorous state of health. We civilized men, on the other hand, do our utmost to check the process of elimination; we build asylums for the imbecile, the maimed and the sick: we institute poor laws and our medical men exert their utmost skill to save the life of every one to the last moment. There is reason to believe that vaccination has preserved thousands who from a weak constitution would formerly have succumbed to smallpox. Thus the weak members of civilized society propagate their kind. No one who has attended to the breeding of domestic animals will doubt that this must be highly injurious to the race of man. It is surprising how soon a want of care, or care wrongly directed, leads to the degeneration of a domestic race; but, excepting in the case of man himself, hardly anyone is so ignorant as to allow his worst animals to breed.
>
> "The aid which we felt impelled to give to the helpless is mainly an incidental result of the instinct of sympathy which was originally acquired as part of the social instincts, but subsequently rendered, in the manner previously indicated, more tender and more widely diffused. Nor could we check our sympathy,

even at the urging of hard reason, without deterioration in the noblest part of our nature? . . . We must therefore bear the undoubtedly bad effects of the weak serving and propagating their kind."

Darwin reveals the barbarous sentiment that runs through evolution and dwarfs the moral nature of those who become obsessed with it. Let us analyze the quotation just given. (71)

---

(71) Again WJB utilizes his specialized brand of polemics. He provides a source, reading in this case Darwin himself, in earlier cases Nietzsche, to the jury. He then isolates "offending" phrases, clauses, or conclusions, highlighting them, then attempts to show the poison in them (from WJB's point of view). In this case, he has chosen one of several passages from Darwin involving social evolution and suggesting solutions that most would find appalling.

Darwin speaks with approval of the savage custom of eliminating the weak so that only the strong will survive, and complains that "we civilized men do our utmost to check the process of elimination." How inhuman such a doctrine as this! He thinks it injurious to "build asylums for the imbecile, the maimed and the sick" or to care for the poor. Even the medical men come in for criticism because they "exert their utmost skill to save the life of everyone to the last moment."

And then note his hostility to vaccination because it has "preserved thousands who, from a weak constitution would, but for vaccination, have succumbed to smallpox!" All of the sympathetic activities of civilized society are condemned because they enable "the weak members to propagate their kind." Then he drags mankind down to the level of the brute and compares the freedom given to man unfavorably with the restraint that we put on barnyard beasts.

The second paragraph of the above quotation shows that his kindly heart rebelled against the cruelty of his own doctrine. He says that we "feel impelled to give to the helpless," although he traces it to a sympathy which he thinks is developed by evolution; he even admits that we could not check this sympathy "even at the urging of hard reason, without deterioration of the noblest part of our nature." "We must therefore bear" what he regards as "the undoubtedly bad effects of the weak surviving and propagating their kind." Could any doctrine be more destructive of civilization? And what a commentary on evolution! He wants us to believe that evolution develops a human sympathy that finally becomes so tender that it repudiates the law that created it and thus invites a return to a level where the extinguishing of pity and sympathy will permit the brutal instincts to again do their progressive (?) work! (72)

(72) The "(?)" appears both in the 1925 Fleming H. Revell edition of this speech and in the appendix of WJB's autobiography, which his wife Mary finished after Bryan's death. The "?" is meant to question the ironic use of "progressive work?"

"Evolution is a Bloody Business"

LET NO ONE think that this acceptance of barbarism as the basic principle of evolution died with Darwin. Within three years a book has appeared whose author is even more frankly brutal than Darwin. The book is entitled *The New Decalogue of Science*[36] and has attracted wide attention. One of our most reputable magazines has recently printed an article by him defining the religion of a scientist. In his preface he acknowledges indebtedness to twenty-one prominent scientists and educators, nearly all of them "doctors" and "professors." One of them, who has recently been elevated to the head of a great state university, read the manuscript over twice "and made many invaluable suggestions."[37] The author describes Nietzsche, who, according to Mr. Darrow, made a murderer out of Babe Leopold, as "the bravest soul since Jesus."[38] He admits that Nietzsche was "gloriously wrong,"[39] not certainly, but "perhaps," "in many details of technical knowledge," but he affirms that "Nietzsche was gloriously right in his fearless questioning of the universe and of his own soul."[40]

In another place, the author says, "Most of our morals today are jungle products,"[41] and then he affirms that "it would be safer, biologically, if they were more so now." After these two samples of his views you will not be surprised when I read you the following (see page 34).

> "Evolution is a bloody business, but civilization tries to make it a pink tea. Barbarism is the only process by which man has ever organically progressed, and civilization is the only process by which he has ever organically declined. Civilization is the most dangerous enterprise upon which man ever set out. For when you take man out of the bloody brutal but beneficent hand of natural selection you place him at once in the soft, perfumed, daintily gloved but far more dangerous hand of artificial selection. And unless you call science to your aid and make this artificial selection as efficient as the rude methods of nature you bungle the whole task."[42]

This aspect of evolution may amaze some of the ministers who have not been admitted to the inner circle of the iconoclasts whose theories menace all the ideals of civilized society. Do these ministers know that "evolution is a bloody business"? Do they know that "barbarism is the only process by which man has ever organically declined"? Do they know that the bloody, brutal hand of natural selection is "beneficent," and that the artificial selection found in civilization is "dangerous"? What shall we think of the distinguished educators and scientists who read the manuscript before publication and did not protest against this pagan doctrine?

Kidd on Darwin and Nietzsche

TO SHOW THAT this is a world-wide matter, I now quote from a book issued from the press in 1918, seven years ago. The title of the book is *The Science of Power*,[43] and its author, Benjamin Kidd, (73) being an Englishman, could not have any national prejudice against Darwin.

---

(73) Benjamin Kidd (1858-1916), British sociologist. His works include *Social Evolution* (1894).

On Pages 46 and 47 we find Kidd's interpretation of evolution:

> "Darwin's presentation of the evolution of the world as the product of natural selection in never-ceasing war—as a product, that is to say, of a struggle in which the individual efficient in the fight for his own interests was always the winning type—touched the profoundest depths of the psychology of the West. The idea seemed to present the whole order of progress in the world as the result of a purely mechanical and materialistic process resting on force. In so doing it was a conception which reached the springs of that heredity born of the unmeasured ages of conquest

out of which the Western mind has come. Within half a century the *Origin of Species* had become the bible of the doctrine of the omnipotence of force."[44]

Kidd goes so far as to charge that "Nietzsche's teaching represented the interpretation of the popular Darwinism delivered with the fury and intensity of genius." [45] And Nietzsche, be it remembered, denounced Christianity as the "doctrine of the degenerate," and democracy as "the refuge of weaklings."

Kidd says that Nietzsche gave Germany the doctrine of Darwin's efficient animal in the voice of his superman, and that Bernhardi and the military textbooks in due time gave Germany the doctrine of the superman translated into the national policy of the super-state aiming at world power.[46] (Page 67.)

And what else but the spirit of evolution can account for the popularity of the selfish doctrine, "each one for himself, and the devil take the hindmost," that threatens the very existence of the doctrine of brotherhood.

In 1900—twenty-five years ago—while an international peace congress was in session in Paris, the following editorial appeared in *L' Univers*:

> "The spirit of peace has fled the earth because evolution has taken possession of it. The plea for peace in past years has been inspired by faith in the divine nature and the divine origin of man; men were

then looked upon as children of one Father, and war, therefore, fratricide. But now that men are looked upon as children of apes what matters it whether they are slaughtered or not?" (74)

---

(74) *L' Univers* was a French based Roman Catholic newspaper. This passage is often quoted in anti-evolution writings but without needed references. Unable to verify.

When there is poison in the blood, no one knows on what part of the body it will break out, but we can be sure that it will continue to break out until the blood is purified. One of the leading universities of the South (I love the State too well to mention its name) published a monthly magazine entitled *Journal of Social Forces*. (75)

---

(75) Most likely WJB is referencing, *Journal of Social Forces* (now Social Forces) published through the Department of Sociology at the University of North Carolina at Chapel Hill. WJB and his wife lived in Asheville, NC from 1917 to 1920.

In the January issue of this year a contributor has a lengthy article on "Sociology and Ethics," in the course of which he says:

> "No attempt will be made to take up the matter of the good or evil of sexual intercourse among humans aside from the matter of conscious procreation, but as an historian it might be worthwhile to ask the exponents of the impurity complex to explain the fact that, without exception the great periods of cultural afflorescence have been those characterized by a large amount of freedom in sex relations, and that those of the greatest cultural degradation and decline have been accompanied with greater sex repression and purity."[47]

No one charges or suspects that all or any large percentage of the advocates of evolution sympathize with this loathsome application of evolution to social life, but it is worthwhile to inquire why those in charge of a great institution of learning allow such filth to be poured out for the stirring of the passions of its students.

Just one more quotation: *The Southeastern Christian Advocate* of June 25, 1925, quotes five eminent college men of Great Britain as joining in an answer to the question "Will civilization survive?" Their reply follows:

> "The greatest danger menacing our civilization is the abuse of the achievements of science. Mastery over the forces of nature has endowed the twentieth century man with a power which he is not fit to exercise. Unless the development of morality catches up with the development of technique, humanity is bound to destroy itself."[48]

Science Not a Teacher of Morals

CAN ANY CHRISTIAN remain indifferent? (76)

---

(76) Much of what follows (as well as some of WJB's previous comments) will seem odd to the reader. Such comments probably would not be allowed in an American courtroom today. WJB moves from summarizing to preaching. Of course, many of the comments and events of the Scopes trial would have been ruled out of order (such as calling WJB of the prosecution to the stand as an expert witness). Such an overtly Christian message was common in the day, especially in the very religious south. Judge Ralston began each day of trial with prayer from a clergyman and kept a Bible on the bench. No one would have thought that out of order—except Darrow who complained bitterly. Of course, this summary was never given. All we have is the published comments and perhaps WJB added some of this material. Most likely, however, he would have given it as published.

Science needs religion, to direct its energies and to inspire with lofty purpose those who employ the forces that are unloosed by science. Evolution is at war with religion because religion is supernatural; it is therefore the relentless foe of Christianity, which is a revealed religion.

Let us, then, hear the conclusion of the whole matter. Science is a magnificent material force, but it is not a teacher of morals. It can perfect machinery, but it adds no moral restraints to protect society from the misuse of the machine. It can also build gigantic intellectual ships, but it constructs no moral rudders or the control of storm-tossed human vessels. It not only fails to supply the spiritual element needed, but some of its unproven hypotheses rob the slip of its compass and thus endanger its cargo. (77)

---

(77) One of the motivating concerns WJB wrestled with was the future where Darwinism replaced morality. Why not war? Why not kill? All people are animals and are free to act like such. WJB would make the same argument today. Eugenics was a natural extension of Darwinism as WJB demonstrated in quoting *Descent of Man*.

In war, science has proven itself an evil genius; it has made war more terrible than it ever was before. (78)

---

(78) WJB was secretary of state under Woodrow Wilson when the United States entered WWI. When he took that position, WJB promised the country that it would not go to war while he held that office. When it did, he felt honor-bound to resign his position. WWI lasted a little over four

years and resulted in the death of nine million combatants and seven million civilians.

Man used to be content to slaughter his fellowmen on a single plain—the earth's surface. Science has taught him to go down into the water and shoot up from below and to go up into the clouds and shoot down from above, (79) thus making the battlefield three times as bloody as it was before.

(79) WWI German U-boats waged unrestricted submarine warfare. WWI was one of the first major wars to use fixed wing aircraft for more than reconnaissance. Fighter aircraft were joined by bombers. The Germans used Zeppelins as well.

But science does not teach brotherly love. Science has made war so hellish that civilization was about to commit suicide; and now we are told that newly discovered instruments of destruction will make the cruelty of the late war seem trivial in comparison with the cruelties of wars that may come in the future. (80)

(80) Chemical weapons were used by all belligerents during the war. As many as 260,000 civilians lost their lives to chemical warfare and 1.2 million people were affected by gas.

If civilization is to be saved from the wreckage threatened by intelligence not consecrated by love, it must be saved by the moral code of the meek and lowly Nazarene. His teachings, and His teachings alone, can solve the problems that vex the heart and perplex the world.

The world needs a Saviour more than it ever did before and there is only one "Name under heaven given among men whereby we must be saved."[49] It is this Name that evolution degrades, for, carried to its logical conclusion, it robs Christ of the glory of a virgin birth, of the majesty of His deity and mission, and of the triumph of His resurrection. It also disputes the doctrine of the atonement. (81)

---

(81) WJB touches on four the of five major points listed as indispensable doctrines by a gathering of fundamentalist church leaders in Niagara-on-the-Lake in Ontario. The list was compiled in 1895. WJB doesn't, in this passage, mention inerrancy but he has already alluded to it several times in this summary and in the trial.

The Issue—God or Baal

IT IS FOR the jury to determine whether this attack upon the Christian religion shall be permitted in the public schools of Tennessee by teachers employed by the State and paid out of the public treasury. (82)

(82) After departing from the original intent of the trial, WJB brings the message back to the original case: Did John T. Scopes willfully violate the Butler Act by teaching, in a public school at state expense, that humans evolved from a lower form of animal life? Although much of the argumentation from the defense and from WJB centered on evolution in schools the fact remained that the case was about a misdemeanor offense.

This case is no longer local: the defendant ceases to play an important part. (83)

(83) Forty years later, Scopes would acknowledge this truth in his autobiography: "At any rate, my own role was a relatively minor one. I furnished the body that was needed to sit in the defendant's chair and, realizing this, I have felt understandably modest about taking credit for what happened in Dayton." John T. Scopes and James Presley, *Center of the Storm: Memoirs of John T. Scopes* (New York: Holt, Rinehart and Winston, 4th printing, 1967), 273.

The case has assumed the proportions of a battle royal between unbelief that attempts to speak through so-called science and the defenders of the Christian faith, speaking through the legislators of Tennessee. It is again a choice between God and Baal; (84) it is also a renewal of the issue in Pilate's court.

---

(84) Baal (sometimes Ba'al) refers to an ancient Phoenician and Canaanite fertility god.

In that historic trial—the greatest in history—force, impersonated by Pilate, occupied the throne. Behind it was the Roman Government, mistress of the world, and behind the Roman Government were the legions of Rome. Before Pilate stood Christ, the apostle of love. Force triumphed; they nailed Him to the tree (85) and those who stood around mocked and jeered and said "He is dead."

---

(85) "Tree" is used in the New Testament as a reference to the Cross of Christ. For example: "Christ redeemed us from the curse of the Law, having become a curse for us—for it is written, 'Cursed is everyone who hangs on a tree' (Galatians 3:13 NASB).

But from that day the power of Caesar waned and the power of Christ increased. In a few centuries the Roman Government was gone and its legions forgotten; while the crucified and risen Lord has become the greatest fact in history and the growing Figure of all time.

Force and Love Meet Face to Face

AGAIN FORCE AND love meet face to face, and the question, "What shall I do with Jesus." must be answered. A bloody, brutal doctrine—evolution—demands, as the rabble did 1,900 years ago, that He be crucified. That cannot be the answer of this jury, representing a Christian state and sworn to uphold the laws of Tennessee. Your answer will be heard throughout the world; it is eagerly awaited by a praying multitude. If the law is nullified, there will be rejoicing wherever God is repudiated, the Saviour scoffed at and the Bible ridiculed. Every unbeliever of every kind and degree will be happy. If, on the other hand, the law is upheld and the religion of the school children protected, millions of Christians will call you blessed and, with hearts full of gratitude to God, will sing again that grand old song of triumph:

> *Faith of our fathers. living still,*
> *In spite of dungeon, fire and sword;*
> *O, how our hearts beat high with joy,*
> *Whene'er we hear that glorious word;*
> *Faith of our fathers—holy faith;*
> *We will be true to thee till death!* (86)

---

(86) "Faith of our Fathers," written by Frederick William Faber (1814-1863) in 1849. A Catholic priest who converted from the Anglican church. This hymn become a favorite of Protestant

churches and is still sung in many churches today.

A BRIEF REPLY BY CLARENCE DARROW

Likens Bryan Speech to Lawyer's Argumentative Statement.

LEXINGTON, Kentucky., July 28 (AP)

CLARENCE DARROW, CHICAGO lawyer who upheld the theory of evolution at the John T. Scopes trial at Dayton, Tenn., tonight answered very briefly the final message of William Jennings Bryan, his chief opponent at the trial.

"I have read what Mr. Bryan intended for his speech at Dayton only hurriedly," Mr. Darrow said, "but it impresses me as only the argumentative statement of a lawyer. He referred again to the Loeb and Leopold case and philosophy of Nietzsche. He indicates that, in his belief such philosophy may have been responsible for their act.

"Loeb knew nothing of evolution or Nietzsche. It is probable he never heard of either. Leopold did, it is true, and had read Nietzsche. But because Leopold had read Nietzsche, does that prove that this philosophy or education was responsible for the act of two crazy boys?

"Isn't it peculiar that of the millions of young men and women who have attended universities and colleges of the country and studied evolution and perhaps Nietzsche, only one of them should commit such a crime as Leopold did?

"If I remember aright, about a week or so after Loeb and Leopold committed their crime a preacher poisoned his wife and a woman her husband that they could be together. Would any one claim that religion had caused this preacher to do the things he did?

"In this world little, if anything, is accomplished without progress. To make Christians of the Chinese you would be forced to kill many of them. The invention of the printing press was frowned upon and even cost some lives, but no one maintains that it has not done good.

"The building of railroads has cost many lives but they aided humanity. Each year automobiles kill more persons than are killed by homicides; but that is no reason they should be abandoned pack and parcel.

"The trial at Dayton has done several things which are significant. Of the jurors who heard the case at Dayton only one of them had ever heard of evolution. Today in Dayton they are selling more books of evolution than any other kind, and the book shops in Chattanooga and other cities of the State are hardly able to supply the demands for works on evolution. The trial has at least started people to thinking."

ABOUT THE AUTHOR

ALTON L. GANSKY is the author of 24 novels, 4 novellas, 1 screenplay, and 10 nonfiction works, as well as principal writer of 9 novels and 2 nonfiction books. He has been a Christy Award finalist (*A Ship Possessed*) and an Angel Award winner (*Terminal Justice*) and recently received the ACFW award for best suspense/thriller for his work on *Fallen Angel*. He holds a BA and MA in biblical studies and was granted a Litt.D. He lives in central California with his wife.

ALLOYD BOOKS is Alton Gansky's publishing venture reissuing his earlier books and publishing new works that may not fit the traditional publishing model.

www.altongansky.com

ENDNOTES

[1] Excerpt from Alton Gansky, *30 Events That Shaped the Church*, (Grand Rapids: Baker Books, 2015), 201-218.

[2] Jeffery P. Moran, *The Scopes Trial: A Brief History with Documents*, (New York: Bedford/St. Martins', 2002) 2.

[3] Paul Amos Moody, *Introduction to Evolution,* New York: Harper & Row, 1970) 492-493.

[4] Lowell Hayes Harrison, *A New History of Kentucky* (Lexington: University Press of Kentucky, 1997) 346.

[5] Quoted in *Nashville Tennessean,* March 24, 1925.

[6] The National Center for Education Statistics, http://nces.ed.gov/programs/digest/d12/tables/dt12_009.asp, Accessed January 15, 2014.

[7] Edward J. Larson, "Before the Crusade: Evolution in American Secondary Education Before 1920," quoted in Moran, *The Scopes Trial.*

[8] "Plan Assault on State Law on Evolution," *Chattanooga Daily Times,* (May 4, 1925) 5.

[9] "Arrest Under Evolution Law," *Nashville Banner* (May 6, 1925) 1.

[10] *Nashville Banner*, "Darrow Ready to Aid Prof. Scopes," May 16, 1925, 1.

[11] *Baltimore Sun*, July 14, 1925, 1.

[12] William Safire, *Lend Me Your Ears: Great Speeches in History* (New York: W.W. & Norton Company, 1997) 849-53.

[13] From the Scopes Trial transcripts.

[14] Quoted in Nan Johnson, *Nineteenth-century Rhetoric in North America*, (Carbondale, IL: Southern University Press, 1991), 247.

[15] John T. Scopes, *Center of the Storm* (New York: Holt, Rinehart and Winston, 1967), 273.

[16] US Supreme Court, *Pierce v. Society of Sisters*, 268 U.S. 510 (1925).

[17] For more information on the "evolution" of Hunter's *A Civic Biology* see Adam R. Shapiro's *Trying Biology*, (Chicago: The University of Chicago Press, 2013), esp. chapters 4-6).

[18] See appendix.

[19] Hunter, *Civic Biology*, 7.

[20] Sir John Arthur Thompson, *Darwinism and Human Life* (New York: Henry Holt and Company, 1911), 9.

[21] Francis Darwin, *Life and Letters of Charles Darwin*, (New York: D. Appleton and Company, 1887), 39.

[22] Francis Darwin, *Life and Letters of Charles Darwin, Vol. 2*, (New York: D. Appleton and Company, 1896), 412.

[23] Francis Darwin, *Life and Letters, Vol. 1*, 277.

[24] Charles Darwin & Francis Darwin (ed.), *Autobiography and Selected Letters* (Mineola (New York): Dover Publications, Inc., 1958), 62.

[25] Darwin, *Autobiography*. 66.

[26] Darwin, *Autobiography*. 70.

[27] George John Romanes, *Thoughts on Religion*, 4th ed. (Chicago: The Open Court Publishing Company, 1898), 180. (page 169 in first edition)

[28] Ramones, *Thoughts on Religion*, 29. (page 28 in the first edition).

[29] Luke 17:1-2 KJV

[30] J. McKeen Cattell, ed., *American Men of Science* (New York: The Science Press, 1906).

[31] Leuba, *Belief in God*, 277.

[32] Leuba, *Belief in God*, 280.

[33] Leuba, *Belief in God*, 280-281.

[34] Matthew 6:10 KJV

[35] Charles Darwin, *The Descent of Man* (London: John Murray, 1871). Page numbers vary depending on publisher and edition.

[36] Albert Edward Wiggam, *The New Decalogue of Science* (Indianapolis: Bobbs-Merril Company, 1922). WJB mentions "One of our most reputable magazines…" The reference is to *The Century Magazine*, (March 1922, vol. 103,) 643-650.

[37] Ibid. 10.

[38] Ibid. 253.

[39] Ibid. 253.

[40] Ibid. 253

[41] Ibid. 102

[42] Ibid. 34

[43] Benjamin Kidd, *The Science of Power* (London: G.P. Putnam's Sons, 1918).

[44] Kidd, The Science of Power, 46-47.

[45] Ibid. 61.

[46] Ibid. 67.

[47] Frank H. Hankins, *Journal of Social Forces*, "Sociology and Ethics: A Genetic View of the Theory of Conduct," January 1925.

[48] Unable to verify.

[49] Acts 4:12 KJV

Made in United States
Orlando, FL
28 December 2022